CULTURES OF THE WORLD
Greece

Cavendish
Square
New York

Published in 2014 by Cavendish Square Publishing, LLC
303 Park Avenue South, Suite 1247, New York, NY 10010

Third Edition

This publication is published with arrangement with Marshall Cavendish International (Asia) Pte Ltd.

Website: cavendishsq.com

Cultures of the World is a registered trademark of Times Publishing Limited.

This publication represents the opinions and views of the author based on his or her personal experience, knowledge, and research. The information in this book serves as a general guide only. The author and publisher have used their best efforts in preparing this book and disclaim liability rising directly or indirectly from the use and application of this book.

CPSIA Compliance Information: Batch #WS13CSQ

All websites were available and accurate when this book was sent to press.

Library of Congress Cataloging-in-Publication Data
Greece / Jill Dubois ... [et al.]. — 3rd ed.
    p. cm. — (Cultures of the world)
  Includes bibliographical references and index.
  ISBN 978-1-60870-869-7 (hardcover) ISBN 978-1-62712-160-6 (paperback) ISBN 978-1-60870-875-8 (ebook)
  1. Greece—Juvenile literature. I. DuBois, Jill, 1952-

  DF717.G779 2014
  949.5—dc23   2012018496

Writers: Jill Dubois, Xenia Skoura, Olga Gratsaniti, and Yong Jui Lin
Editors: Deborah Grahame-Smith, Mindy Pang
Copyreader: Tara Tomczyk
Designers: Nancy Sabato, Adithi
Cover picture researcher: Tracey Engel
Picture researcher: Joshua Ang

PICTURE CREDITS
Cover: © Vidler / age footstock
Banknotes.com 135 • Getty Images 103 • Inmagine.com 1, 3, 5, 6, 9, 10, 12, 15, 16, 18, 20, 21, 22, 23, 24, 26, 27, 28, 29, 30, 32, 34, 35, 37, 38, 40, 43, 44, 45, 46, 48, 50, 51, 52, 53, 54, 55, 56, 59, 61, 62, 64, 66, 68, 69, 70, 71, 72, 73, 74, 76, 77, 78, 79, 80, 81, 82, 84, 85, 87, 89, 91, 92, 94, 95, 97, 98, 99, 100, 101, 102, 104, 105, 106, 107, 108, 109, 110, 111, 112, 113, 114, 115, 116, 117, 118, 119, 120, 121, 122, 123, 124, 125, 126, 127, 128, 129, 130, 131

PRECEDING PAGE
A church with the bell tower stands by a coast in Santorini, part of the Cyclades islands.

Printed in the United States of America

CONTENTS

GREECE TODAY

THE STATE OF MODERN GREECE HAS EXISTED FOR 52 YEARS fewer than the United States; it was founded in 1828, following the Greek War of Independence, when the Great Powers (the United Kingdom, France, and Russia) had given the recognition of its autonomy from the ruling Ottoman Empire.

Modern Greece traces its roots to the civilization of ancient Greece, generally considered the cradle of Western civilization. As such, Greek civilization is the birthplace of democracy, Western philosophy, the Olympic Games, Western literature, political science, major scientific and mathematical principles, and Western drama, including both tragedy and comedy. This legacy is partly reflected in the 17 United Nations Educational, Scientific and Cultural Organization (UNESCO) World Heritage Sites located in Greece, ranking Greece seventh in Europe and 13th in the world in terms of the number of UNESCO sites.

At its geographical peak, Greek civilization spread from Greece to Egypt and to the Hindu Kush Mountains in Afghanistan. Since then, Greek minorities have remained in former Greek territories, and Greek emigrants have assimilated into societies across the globe.

The Vikos Gorge lies in the North Pindus Mountains in the region of Epirus, 24 miles (39 km) from the Albanian border. This 7-mile (11 km) gorge is part of the Aoos-Vikos National Park and is popular with hikers.

The traditional date for the end of the ancient Greek period is the death of Alexander the Great in 323 B.C. The period that follows is classified as Hellenistic. Hellenistic civilization has been immensely influential on the language, politics, educational systems, philosophy, art, and architecture of the modern world, particularly during the Renaissance in Western Europe and again during various neoclassical revivals in 18th- and 19th-century Europe and the Americas.

Romans conquered ancient Greece in 168 B.C., but Greek culture conquered Roman life. With the Christianization of Greece following the Byzantine Empire's formation in A.D. 395, the Greek peninsula became one of the strongest centers of Christianity. In 1453, after an invasion, Greece became part of the Ottoman Empire.

Greece consists of a mountainous, peninsular mainland jutting out into the sea at the southern end of the Balkans, ending at the Peloponnese Peninsula (separated from the mainland by the canal of the Isthmus of Corinth). Greece also has 1,200 islands, of which 227 are inhabited. Crete is the largest and most populous island; Euboea, separated from the mainland by the 197-feet-wide (60-meter-wide) Euripus Strait, is the second largest, followed by Rhodes and Lesbos.

Eighty percent of Greece consists of mountains or hills, making the country one of the most mountainous in Europe. Mount Olympus, the mythical abode of the Greek gods, is the highest in the country. The Pindus mountain range is characterized by its high, steep peaks, often dissected by numerous canyons. The spectacular Vikos Gorge, part of the Vikos-Aoos National Park in the Pindus Mountains, is listed by Guinness World Records as the deepest gorge in the world. Other notable formations are the Meteora rock pillars, atop which were built medieval Greek Orthodox monasteries. Rare marine species such as the pinniped seal and the loggerhead sea turtle live in the seas surrounding mainland Greece, while its dense forests are home to the endangered brown bear, the lynx, the roe deer, and the wild goat.

Greece has been a member of the North Atlantic Treaty Organization (NATO) since 1952, what is now the European Union (EU) since 1981, and the eurozone since 2001, and it is a founding member of the United Nations. Greece is a developed country with an advanced economy and relatively comfortable standards of living. However, since late 2007, the Greek economy has been hit by severe economic and financial crisis, resulting in the Greek government requesting €240 billion ($302 billion) in loans from EU institutions, a substantial debt write-off, stringent austerity measures, and political instability. In 2012 Greece secured a second economic bailout package worth €130 billion ($173 billion). Moreover, its economy was expected to shrink for a sixth straight year in 2013, stagnate in 2014, and only modestly expand in 2015.

The Greek debt is the biggest sovereign debt default in history, accumulated to gargantuan proportions—160 percent of gross domestic product (GDP)—during some 30 years of irresponsible spending. Greece cannot afford to service the interest on this debt, much less repay the capital. Up until the late 1970s, Greece was still considered a miracle economy. For most of the period between the mid-1950s and the mid-1970s, its economic growth was compared with that of Japan. Its accession to what was then the European Communities as its 10th member (even before Spain and Portugal) was not only politically motivated; it was also based on this impressive growth spurt.

Corruption in Greece is so bad that it has been estimated that €30 billion, or 12 percent of GDP, are lost to tax cheats every year. The black market now makes up one-third of the Greek economy. Greece also has lower wages compared with other European member states. As a result, many Greeks work the "black employment market," with no taxes or payments to insurance and pension funds, just so they can get higher wages.

Greece is entering its sixth year of economic crisis and, increasingly, Greek society is unravelling at the seams. The official unemployment rate has exceeded 20%, exacerbated by the austerity measures being pushed through in return for more bailout money. The suicide rate in Greece has reached a pan-European high, with experts attributing the rise to the country's economic crisis. Statistics released by the Greek Ministry of Health show a 40 percent increase in those taking their own lives between January and May 2011 compared with the same period in 2010. Psychiatrists have reported a 30 percent increase in demand for their services in 2012, with most patients citing anxiety and depression brought on by financial fears. Homelessness has soared by an estimated 25 percent since 2009 as Greece spirals further into its worst postwar economic crisis. Most heartbreaking of all, families are abandoning children because they cannot afford to raise them. Children's homes are now filled with not only victims of abuse but victims of the economic crisis as well.

Tourism has been hailed as the answer that could revive the moribund Greek economy, accounting almost a fifth of the country's gross domestic product. However, the economic crisis has also hit the Greek tourism sector. From the rolling hills of Arcadia to the plains of Macedonia to the sunbaked palaces of Crete, examples of the thwarted efforts of cash-strapped Greek authorities to showcase Greece's historical wealth are common.

However, the government has made measures to boost tourism. In 2011 the government got rid of visa requirements for non-EU citizens, waived landing and takeoff fees for aircraft at airports nationwide, and took steps to facilitate foreign investment. In the tourism sector, like so many others, has been afflicted by corruption, cronyism, and lack of competitiveness—the very ills that helped bring Greece to its knees. These measures appear to be paying off. To reverse several lean years, Greece braced for a turnaround in 2012 in terms of tourism, with popular Ionian islands, such as Zákintho reporting an increase in the number of visitors in 2012. Unfortunately, sporadic strikes, riots, political instability and a fluctuating currency dampened visitor arrivals to Athens in 2012. To address this problem, the Greek National Tourism Organization (GNTO) launched a campaign called "True Greece" in 2012 to spruce up the country's negative image in the international media.

In March 2007 the Acropolis was formally proclaimed the preeminent monument on the European Cultural Heritage list of monuments. The Acropolis is a flat-topped rock that rises 492 feet (150 meters) above sea level in the city of Athens, with a surface area of about 7.4 acres (3 hectares).

All the valuable ancient artifacts are situated in the Acropolis Museum, which resides on the southern slope of the same rock, 919 feet (280 m) from the Parthenon. The Parthenon is a temple on the Acropolis dedicated to the Greek goddess Athena, whom the people of Athens considered their patron.

The ancient Greece of Olympia was the site of the Olympic Games in classical times, comparable in importance to the Pythian Games held in Delphi. The Olympic Games were held every four years, dating back to 776 B.C. The first Olympic Games were in honor of Zeus; Emperor Theodosius I abolished them in A.D. 394, as they were then considered a relic of paganism. The sanctuary in Olympia, known as the Altis, consists of an unordered arrangement of various buildings. Enclosed within the sacred enclosure are the Temple of Hera and the Temple of Zeus, the Pelopion, and the area of the altar where the sacrifices were made.

The site of Delphi is located in lower central Greece, on multiple plateaus and terraces along the slope of Mount Parnassus, and includes the Sanctuary of Apollo, the site of the ancient Oracle. Southwest of Delphi, about 19.3 miles (31 kilometers) away, is the harbor city of Kirrha on the Corinthian Gulf. Delphi was thought of by the Greeks as the center of the entire planet.

Tourists by the Propylaea (or entrance) to the Acropolis in Athens. The Propylaea was completed in fifth century B.C., just before the outbreak of the Peloponnesian Wars. It was during the reign of Pericles that the four masterpieces of classical Greek art were built—the main temple dedicated to Athena, the Parthenon; the Temple of Athena Nike; the Erechtheion, and the Propylaea.

GEOGRAPHY

The village of Oia, on the Greek island of Santorini, is a popular tourist destination and home to a large, dormant, caldera volcano—Santorini. The volcano of Santorini caused one of the most violent volcanic eruptions in history, some 3,600 years ago. That eruption, which created tsunamis 40 feet (12 m) tall, is said to have spawned the legend of the lost city of Atlantis. Santorini last erupted in 1950 but on a much smaller scale.

GREECE LIES AT THE CROSSROADS of three continents. The country is located at the southeastern corner of Europe on the southern part of the Balkan Peninsula. Asia lies to the east of Greece, and Africa lies south across the Mediterranean Sea.

Greece is nearly surrounded by water. The farthest inland point in Greece is only about 50 miles (80.5 km) from the sea. The country is bordered by the Aegean Sea on the east, the Mediterranean Sea on the south, and the Ionian Sea on the west. In the north, Greece shares a boundary with Albania, the former Yugoslavian republic of Macedonia, and Bulgaria. Its neighbor in the northeast and across the Aegean Sea is Turkey.

With an area of 50,949 square miles (131,958 square km), Greece is about the same size as England or Alabama. About one-fifth of the total Greek land area consists of at least 1,200 islands scattered across the country's surrounding seas. About 227 of these islands are inhabited, whereas others are merely rocky outcrops. Greece is famous for its jagged coastline, which totals about 8,498 miles (13,676 km) in length—the 11th-longest coastline in the world.

LAND OF MOUNTAINS

Greece is a mountainous country. Rugged mountains cover three-fourths of the Greek mainland. The Pindus Mountains run from Albania and the Republic of Macedonia in the north through northeastern and central Greece and on to the Peloponnese in the south.

Cargo ship being pulled down the Corinth Canal. Due to the canal's narrowness and landslips, it is primarily used for tourist traffic.

The areas lying between the mountain ranges form the Greek lowlands, which account for just 20 percent of Greek territory. These flat plains are located mainly along the coast, between the mountains and the sea. Other lowlands include mountain basins and valleys that have been cultivated and flatlands near river deltas.

Mainland Greece is divided into seven regions: Macedonia (not to be confused with the country to the north), Thrace, Epirus, Thessaly, Central Greece (also called Sterea Ellas), Attica, and the Peloponnese.

Epirus, on the northwestern corner of the Greek peninsula bordering Albania, is the most mountainous region. Thessaly, however, is home to the highest mountain in Greece, Mount Olympus. Prominent in ancient Greek literature and mythology, it rises to 9,570 feet (2,917 m).

The Peloponnese is a large peninsula, joined to the rest of mainland Greece by a narrow strip of land called the Isthmus of Corinth. Starting with Periander, ruler of Corinth in seventh century B.C., many have attempted to construct a canal to connect the Gulf of Corinth with the Aegean Sea's Saronic Gulf. A canal that cut through the Isthmus of Corinth would separate the Peloponnesian peninsula from the Greek mainland, shortening the journey of ships moving between the Western Mediterranean or the Adriatic and the Eastern Mediterranean or the Black Sea by as much as 248 miles (400 km). However, the Corinth Canal was only completed at the end of the 19th century.

The Greek islands are spread across the Ionian and Aegean seas. Crete, Greece's largest island, has an area of 3,218 square miles (8,335 square km) and lies in the Mediterranean at the entrance to the Aegean Sea.

The Ionian Islands include Corfu, Levkás, Cephalonia, Zákinthos, Ithaca, Paxos, Kíthera, and smaller satellite islands.

The Aegean Islands are more numerous—they include Samothrace, Lemnos, and Lesbos in the north; the Sporades in the west; the Cyclades in the center; and Samos, Rhodes, and the Dodecanese Islands in the southeast. Many of the islands are also mountainous; for instance, the mountains of Crete are part of the Pindus mountain range. The Santorini archipelago was the site of the second largest volcanic eruption in history 3,600 years ago. The explosion is likely to have destroyed the Minoan civilization based in nearby Crete.

RIVERS AND LAKES

Greece has few rivers and lakes. None of the rivers are navigable, because of the mountainous terrain, so they are not used for transporting people or goods. Many of the smaller rivers even dry up in the summer. The most important rivers in Greece include the Achelous, the Peneus, the Vardar (also known as the Axiós), and the Strymon.

The country's largest lakes are located in the northern region. They include Ioánnina, Kastoria, and Prespa.

FLORA AND FAUNA

Many flowers, shrubs, and trees can be found throughout Greece, including tulips, laurels, acacias, bougainvilleas, hibiscuses, jasmines, mimosas, oleanders, and sycamores. Greece has about 6,000 species of wildflowers. Anemones, poppies, and cyclamens are found in areas above 4,000 feet (1,219 m), while mosses and lichens grow in regions above 5,000 feet (1,524 m). Plants that tolerate Greece's stony soil include thyme, bellflowers, grape hyacinths, stars of Bethlehem, and yarrows.

About 30 percent of Greece is covered in forest. In the north and at higher altitudes, coniferous forests of Grecian fir and black pine thrive. Deciduous trees such as oak and chestnut grow at lower altitudes. Pines, planes, and poplars also thrive along Greece's rocky slopes and coastal plains.

Among the wildlife found in the forested regions, especially in the north, are the brown bear, the wildcat, the chamois (a goatlike antelope), the deer, the fox, the badger, and the weasel. Wolves and lynx are becoming rare. Farther south, jackals, foxes, wild goats, and porcupines are found.

On August 2, 1913, Swiss climbers Fred Boissonas and Daniel Baud Bovy and local guide Christos Kakkalos were the first people to make it to the summit of Mount Olympus.

The port of Piraeus is the chief port in Greece, the largest passenger port in Europe, and the third-largest passenger port in the world, servicing about 20 million passengers annually.

Many birds from northern and central Europe migrate to Greece for the winter. Among the birds of Greece are the hawk, the eagle, the egret, the nightingale, the partridge, the pheasant, the pelican, the stork, and the turtledove.

One of Greece's most interesting creatures is found in the sea: a shellfish called the murex, which was used thousands of years ago to produce a purple dye for coloring the clothing of wealthy people. Other marine creatures include octopuses, which live along the shore, hiding behind rocks to protect their soft bodies from marine predators. Octopuses range in size from very tiny to more than 14 feet (4.3 m) across. Even larger are squids, which can grow as long as 75 feet (23 m). Other common animals found in the warm waters of the Mediterranean are dolphins, seals, and turtles. Some species of sea turtles are in danger of extinction.

CITIES

More than 40 percent of the population lives in the capital, Athens (called Athina in Greek). Overall, about 61 percent of Greeks live in urban areas. Although small in comparison with the Greek capital, other urban centers such as Thessaloníki, Patras, Volos, Larissa, and Iráklion (also known as Heraklion) on the island of Crete have grown rapidly since the 1990s.

ATHENS Athens is the political and commercial hub of Greece. It lies in a valley among three mountains—Pendelikón, Hymettus, and Parnitha. The city is centered on two hills, the Acropolis and Lycabettus.

Although Athens was the center of Greek civilization for more than 5,000 years, it has been the capital of Greece only since 1834.

During the Turkish occupation of Greece from 1453 to 1812, Athens declined in importance as Constantinople (now Istanbul, a city in Turkey) attracted more trade. By the time Greece gained independence in 1821, Athens had been reduced to a sprawling village. Since becoming the capital of independent Greece, the population of Athens has risen from 10,000 in 1834 to 3.07 million in 2011.

The city of Athens has grown so much since the end of World War II that its traditional boundaries have been stretched to the port of Piraeus, 6 miles (10 km) from the city center. One of the largest ports in the Mediterranean, Piraeus has a population of 880,000 and is home to Greece's merchant navy, one of the largest in the world. More than half of Greece's manufacturing industry is located here. Piraeus is a vital industrial area, with hundreds of factories producing tobacco products, fertilizers, cloth, and chemicals.

Rapid growth in the capital, however, has produced urban problems. Poor city planning has resulted in little open space in Athens, as buildings erected in the past 40 years are too close to one another. There are also few trees to provide shade and beautify the streets. Pollution has also become a serious problem, especially with the increasing number of vehicles in the city. The combination of vehicle exhaust and industrial smoke produces an acidic smog that gets trapped inside the city by the mountains encircling Athens. This acidic smog, in the form of acid rain, eats away marble. Thus, a major concern about the smog is the harm it is causing to the city's ancient monuments, most of which are made from marble.

Piraeus is Greece's biggest port and is also an important center for industry and transportation.

THESSALONÍKI

The second-largest city in Greece, with a population of about 1 million, Thessaloníki is often called "the northern capital." It was founded in 315 B.C. by Kassandros, an army general who married Thessaloníki, Alexander the Great's stepsister.

Thessaloníki is circled by low hills facing an open bay. Because of its strategic location on the Aegean Sea, the city has been a prime target for invaders since ancient times. During the Turkish occupation of Greece, Thessaloníki outranked Athens in commercial and cultural importance. At the beginning of the 21st century, Thessaloníki was the second most important port and city in Greece.

Among Thessaloníki's many monuments is a triumphal arch erected in A.D. 303 by the Romans to honor Emperor Galerius. Via Egnatia was also built by the Romans, to link Constantinople with Rome. After undergoing renovation in recent times, Via Egnatia continues to serve as the city's main road. Some Greek Christian art from the Byzantine era still survives in the city's churches.

PATRAS

The third largest city in Greece and the main city of the Peloponnese, Patras has a population of 222,460. It is the most important shipping center in western Greece, with ferry and container-shipping links to the Ionian Islands and Italy. The south-western port of Patras has a population of 300,000. Patras is also an important export center for currants, or dried Corinth raisins, which are shipped to Europe.

The Rion-Antirion Bridge is the world's longest multi-span cable-stayed bridge, with a suspended deck longer than 1 mile (2 km). It crosses the Gulf of Corinth near Patras, linking the town of Rio on the Peloponnese to Antirio on mainland Greece. Completed in 2004, some 10,000 vehicles cross it daily.

CLIMATE

Greece has three well-defined climatic areas: Mediterranean, Alpine, and mid-European temperate. It is hot and dry in the summer, but cool sea breezes make the heat bearable. Varying ranges of altitude and closeness to the sea, however, do result in differences in climate.

In the lowlands, summers are hot and dry, and winters are generally cold and damp. The average winter temperature in Athens is 50°F (10°C), but it can be colder in other parts of the country. In the northern region of Thessaloníki, the average temperature in January is 43°F (6°C). The colder northern climate is partly due to the bora, an icy wind that originates in the Balkan regions. Frost and snow are rare in the lowlands, but the mountains are covered with snow in the winter.

On the southern coast of Crete, it is warm enough to swim almost every day, and summer temperatures can reach 90°F (32°C). Still, snow remains on Crete's highest mountains all year round. The northern regions of Thrace, Macedonia, and Thessaly enjoy slightly cooler summers.

Rainfall also varies from region to region. Thessaly can have as little as 1.5 inches (3.8 centimeters) of rainfall per year, while parts of the western coast receive as much as 50 inches (127 cm) of rain per year.

The mountain ranges of Greece have served as a natural barrier against foreign invasion. They have also limited the amount of land available for farming.

INTERNET LINKS

www.greeka.com/greece-geography.htm

This website provides a good guide to the Greek Islands with pictures.

www.ancientgreece.com/s/Geography/

This is a fascinating guide to the geography of ancient Greece.

www.crystalinks.com/greekgeography.html

This website is an interesting guide to Greek geography with intriguing pictures of the country.

HISTORY

The restored Temple of Hephaestus, located on Kolonos Agoraios hill overlooking the Agora in Athens. It was built around 449 B.C., commissioned by the Athenian politician Pericles, and contains cult statues of Athena and Hephaestus.

2

GREECE IS AN ANCIENT COUNTRY with a rich history of cultural and intellectual achievement. The remains of prehistoric humans, dating back almost 100,000 years, have been discovered here. Ancient Greek civilization has been immensely influential on the language, politics, educational systems, philosophy, art, and architecture of the modern world, particularly during the Renaissance in Western Europe and again during various neoclassical revivals in 18th- and 19th-century Europe and the Americas.

EARLY CIVILIZATIONS

THE CYCLADIC CIVILIZATION Based in the Cyclades, this Bronze Age civilization flourished from 3000 to 1000 B.C. It was destroyed by a volcanic eruption on the island of Santorini around 1500 B.C.

THE MINOAN CIVILIZATION The Minoan civilization (3000—1450 B.C.) was centered on the island of Crete. Named after King Minos, this civilization was a peaceful sea power that traded with Syria, Spain, Egypt, and mainland Greece. The Minoans were sophisticated

At its peak, Greek civilization spread from Greece to Egypt and to the Hindu Kush Mountains in Afghanistan. Since then, Greek minorities have remained in former Greek territories (such as Turkey, Albania, Italy, Libya, Armenia, and Georgia), and Greek emigrants have assimilated into differing societies across the globe (including North America, Australia, northern Europe, and South Africa).

people who built beautiful cities and made use of technology unknown in neighboring cultures. The palace at Knossos, a Minoan city in Crete, had an indoor plumbing system.

The Minoan civilization came to an abrupt end around 1500 B.C., when a volcanic eruption in Santorini destroyed Knossos and other Minoan cities. The eruption did not completely wipe out Minoan culture, however. By this time, Minoan influence in architecture and the arts had spread to the Greek mainland.

THE MYCENAEAN CIVILIZATION The Mycenaean civilization lasted from 1600 to 1100 B.C. and was based on the Peloponnese Peninsula with Mycenae as the center of power.

The Mycenaeans were an advanced civilization. They built palaces and were skilled artisans. Many artifacts, such as daggers, shields, death masks, and drinking cups, have been uncovered from Mycenaean ruins.

The Iliad, Homer's epic story, tells of the Trojan War between the Greeks and the kingdom of Troy in Asia Minor. This war began when Paris, the prince of Troy, kidnapped Helen, the wife of the king of Sparta. Agamemnon, king of Mycenae, fought in this war, which eventually ended with the capture of Troy. It is believed this long war contributed to the collapse of the Mycenaean civilization around 1100 B.C.

The Greeks call this period of Mycenaean culture the Heroic Age of Greece, in honor of the Mycenaeans' courage.

THE DARK AGES The downfall of the Mycenaeans was brought about by the Dorians, a tribe from northern Greece. The Dorians used iron weapons that were superior to the bronze arms of the Mycenaeans.

The Dorian invasion was the beginning of an era of instability in Greece that lasted until about 800 B.C. Farming was in a state of disorder, trade was almost nonexistent, and there was a general decline in the arts. This period of Greek history is known as the Dark Ages of Greece.

The Delphi archaeological site is a World Heritage Site. Built on the slopes of Mount Parnassos, it is home to an Archaeological Museum where antique statues are restored. The treasure trove of monuments at Delphi include: the Sanctuary of Apollo, the Sacred Way, the Sanctuary of Athena and a fourth-century theatre and stadium.

THE CITY-STATES

The rise of the city-state, or polis, around 800 B.C. brought an end to the Dark Ages and marked the beginning of the Archaic Period.

City-states developed after isolated villages banded together under the authority of a particular city. Each city-state had its own system of government, industry, commerce, and culture. Corinth, Athens, Thebes, Delphi, Sparta, and Olympia were important city-states.

The Archaic Period was followed by the Classical Period, which lasted from 500 to 336 B.C. During this period Greek arts and sciences reached a high standard of achievement. The city-states were also the birthplace of the world's first democracies. The early city-states were ruled by kings. After 500 B.C., however, democratic governments developed, and free male citizens were allowed to serve in the government of the city-states.

During the Archaic Period, the city-states faced the threat of invasion from the Persian Empire in Asia Minor. In 490 B.C. King Darius of Persia fought the city-state of Athens on the plains of Marathon. Although the Persian army outnumbered the Athenians by almost four to one, the Athenians defeated the Persians, who lost more than 6,000 men whilst the Greeks lost fewer than 200.

In 480 B.C. all the city-states united under the leadership of Athens and again defeated the Persians in the battles of Salamis and Plataea. These Greek victories wiped out any future threat of Persian invasion.

THE GOLDEN AGE OF ATHENS

Athens emerged as the political and cultural center of Greece following the defeat of the Persians. In the peaceful years that followed, democracy and the arts flourished. Athenian accomplishments in science, the arts, philosophy, and architecture during the sixth to eighth centuries B.C., called the Golden Age of Athens, set the standard for later European civilizations.

The Golden Age of Greek literature was marked by Hesiod's poems and Homer's epic poems *The Iliad* and *The Odyssey.* Greek theater reached great heights with the Athenian tragedies of Aeschylus, Sophocles, and Euripides and the comedies of Aristophanes.

In architecture, many beautiful structures, such as the Parthenon of Athens, were built. This was also the age of great philosophers. Socrates and Plato devoted their lives to the pursuit of truth and knowledge. Aristotle, Plato's student, made enormous contributions to science and philosophy.

Athenian supremacy was later challenged by Sparta, a rival city-state. In 431 B.C., the Peloponnesian Wars broke out between the city-states. The wars lasted 27 years. Athens was defeated, and Sparta ruled Greece for a short time. Sparta was later defeated by the city-state of Thebes, which was quickly overthrown. The wars greatly weakened the Greek city-states.

MACEDONIA

In the middle of the fourth century B.C., King Phillip II of Macedon in northern Greece attacked and captured the weakened Greek city-states. Phillip greatly

Statue of Plato at the Academy of Athens. Plato was Socrates's disciple. In 387 B.C., he founded a school of learning which he called the Academy. Perhaps the first European university, its curriculum included astronomy, biology, mathematics, political theory, and philosophy.

admired the cultural developments of the city-states; his goal was to build a huge Greek army and spread Greek civilization to other lands, such as Persia. Phillip was assassinated in 336 B.C. before he could realize this dream.

Phillip's son Alexander carried on his father's plans and became one of the greatest soldiers and conquerors in history. Although he came to the throne at the age of 20 and ruled for only 13 years, Alexander the Great created one of the largest empires in the ancient world. Thanks to Aristotle's tutorship and his own military genius, Alexander the Great conquered the vast Persian Empire, Egypt, and lands as far east as northern India.

The success of Alexander's campaigns was mostly due to his cavalry, a group of about 5,000 armed horsemen. A military formation called the phalanx—a solid, moving wall of foot soldiers bearing shields and long spears—also played an important role in his victories. Alexander's father, Phillip, had also used the phalanx to defeat the city-states.

After Alexander died in 323 B.C. at the age of 33, his great empire collapsed. Parts of his empire became independent city-states. Other parts became independent kingdoms, such as Syria, Egypt, and Macedonia. Alexander's legacy, however, lived on in the city of Alexandria in Egypt, which became a center of learning. By the time of Alexander's death, Greek culture had spread to almost all the lands that he had conquered. After Alexander's death, Macedonia controlled Greece for 200 years.

Ancient Greek warriors were called hoplites, after their shield–the *hoplon*. *Hoplon*s were made of bronze-covered wood, spanning 3-3.5 feet (0.9-1 m) in diameter, spanning from chin to knee and weighing 17-33 pounds (7.7-15 kg).

ROMAN AND BYZANTINE EMPIRES

In 146 B.C., the powerful Roman Empire conquered Greece. The Greeks welcomed the Romans, whom they regarded as the "protectors of Greek freedom." The Romans treated the Greeks with respect out of their great

The Hagia Sophia, in present-day Istanbul, was originally built as a Christian cathedral, a domed basilica. In the 15th century, it was converted to a Muslim mosque–Ayasofya Mosque, and it is now a museum. The grand dome of the Hagia Sophia is an impressive technical feat for its time.

admiration for Greek intellectual and cultural life. Greece prospered once again, and Greek art and culture continued to thrive during this period.

Roman culture was greatly influenced by Greek culture. In mythology, the Roman gods were based on the Greek gods. When Christianity spread, the Greeks were among the first converts, and the Gospels were first written in Greek.

In A.D. 285, Emperor Diocletian decided to share the throne of the vast Roman Empire. He ruled the eastern half of the empire and appointed another emperor to rule the western half. Although in theory the empire was still one, in practice it had become divided. The western half was Latin-speaking, while the eastern half was Greek-speaking.

Constantine succeeded Diocletian in A.D. 312. In A.D. 324 Constantine moved the capital of the empire from Rome to the city of Byzantium. The western empire fell to Germanic tribes in 476. The eastern empire flourished independently and came to be known as the Byzantine Empire.

THE BYZANTINE EMPIRE After the death of Emperor Constantine, Byzantium was renamed Constantinople in his honor. For nearly nine centuries, from 330 to 1204, Constantinople remained the capital of the Byzantine Empire. The empire was Greek in culture and language, but its laws and administration were based on Roman practices.

In 394 Emperor Theodosius I declared Christianity the official religion in Greece and forbade the worship of Greek and Roman gods, which he regarded as paganism.

Justinian the Great (ruled 527—565) was the most famous Byzantine emperor. He wanted to restore the former glory of the ancient Roman Empire to the Byzantine Empire. Although the empire under his control was far smaller than that of ancient Rome, he was able to expand his control to northern Africa, Italy, and parts of Spain. Under Justinian's rule, Christian theology replaced the study of classical Greek philosophy as the highest form of scholarship. Beautiful churches, such as the Hagia Sophia, or Great Church, in Constantinople, were built during this time.

FRANKISH AND VENETIAN OCCUPATION

In 1204 the fourth crusade from Europe tore the Byzantine Empire apart. Constantinople was plundered, and the Aegean Islands and the Greek mainland fell to the Frankish crusaders and their Venetian allies.

Although Constantinople was freed 55 years later, much of Greece and the Aegean Islands remained under Frankish and Venetian occupation. Greece was divided into small states controlled by various Frankish and Venetian administrators.

By the mid-1400s the Ottoman Turks from Anatolia (now in Turkey) had advanced on Greece, conquering each of the city-states. In 1453 Constantinople was captured by the Turks, marking the end of the Byzantine Empire and the beginning of the Turkish domination of Greece.

TURKISH RULE

The Turkish occupation of all of Greece lasted from 1453 to 1821, although Turks continued to rule parts of Greece until 1912. The Turks were Muslims but allowed religious freedom. They were especially tolerant of Jews and Christians, whom they referred to as "People of the Book," people who worshipped one God and had a written scripture. The Turks were more tolerant of other religions than the Roman Catholic Franks and Venetians had been. Turkish rule, however, was oppressive. The Turks imposed heavy taxes, which unpaid would lead to enslavement or death; forced one out of every five male Greek children to enlist in the Turkish army after converting him to Islam; took away girls to work as chambermaids; killed groups of Greek men they thought might lead a revolution; and engaged in numerous wars with Venice, using Greece as a battleground.

The Greeks living in the plains during Ottoman domination were either Christians who dealt with the burdens of foreign rule or Crypto-Christians (Greek Muslims who were secret practitioners of the Greek Orthodox faith). Some Greeks became Crypto-Christians to avoid heavy taxes and at the same time express their identity by maintaining their ties to the Greek Orthodox Church.

Equestrian statue of King Constantine I (1868-1923) in Areos Park, Athens. He led the Greek army during the unsuccessful Greco-Turkish War of 1897 and was Crown Prince during the victorious Balkan Wars of 1912-13, in which Greece captured Thessaloníki and doubled in area and population.

The Greeks suffered poverty under Turkish rule and many Greeks had to resort to farming to survive. Turkish oppression, however, led to the strengthening of Greek ethnic pride. Greek culture, language, and beliefs were preserved by the Eastern Orthodox Church, and the Church came to represent Greek nationalism.

INDEPENDENCE

By the 1820s the Turkish Ottoman Empire was losing control of its vast territory. In 1821 the Greeks began a revolt that eventually led to the Greek War of Independence. In 1827 French, Russian, and British forces joined Greece in its fight against the Turks. Following the destruction of the Ottoman and Egyptian fleets in the Navarino harbor on 20 October 1827, the Turkish sultan signed a treaty recognizing Greek independence in 1829.

BIRTH OF MODERN GREECE

In 1830 the Great Powers, or the Allies—Britain, France, and Russia, signed the London Protocol. The treaty declared the independence of Greece, under a monarchy and established a Greek kingdom made up of the mainland south of Thessaly, the Peloponnese, the Aegean Islands, and the island of Euboea. In order to avoid a power struggle among the Greeks, the Great Powers decided to appoint a foreign king, Prince Leopold of Saxe-Coburg, as Prince-Sovereign of Greece.

In 1833 Prince Otto of Bavaria was crowned king of Greece. Although popular at the start of his reign, Otto later lost the support of the Greek people and was deposed in 1862. The Great Powers replaced him with Prince William of Denmark, who was crowned King George I, and a new liberal and democratic constitution was enacted.

King George I regained Greece's traditional territory with the acquisition of the Ionian Islands from the British, as well as Thessaly and southern Epirus from the Ottoman Turks. In 1912, after emerging victorious in the Balkan Wars, Greece reclaimed Epirus, Macedonia, Crete, and several islands.

King George I was assassinated in 1913. His successor, King Constantine, disagreed with his charismatic prime minister, Eleutherios Venizélos, over Greece's role in World War I. The rivalry between king and prime minister divided the Greek population into two—one side supporting Constantine, and the other Venizélos. Constantine turned to Germany for help, given the real threat of civil war in 1916, but without success. Meanwhile, the Allies threatened to invade Greece (sponsored by Venizélos) unless Constantine abdicated. Constantine had no choice but to step down and, under Venizélos's authority, Greece joined the war in 1917 on the side of the Allies. Over the next 18 months, some 5,000 Greek soldiers would die on the battlefields of World War I.

French troops parading in Salonica (old name for Thessaloníki or Thessalonica) on Greek Independence Day, 1916, during World War I.

DICTATORSHIP AND WAR

King Constantine returned to power in 1920 with much public support. The victory of the Allies and the defeat of the Ottoman Turks in World War I granted Greece the opportunity to reclaim territory from Turkey. However, the Greeks were bitterly defeated by the Turks in Anatolia in 1922. The king was blamed for this defeat and forced into exile. His son and successor, King George II, reigned until 1924, when Greece became a republic for a short period. In 1935 King George II was called back, as many Greeks still supported the monarchy.

With the king's consent, a military dictator, Ioánnis Metaxas, suspended the constitution in August 1936 and ruled Greece until 1940. When Italy invaded Greece during World War II, Greek forces, under Alexandros Papagos, drove back the much larger Italian army. The Greek army, however, was unable to hold off the German invasion in 1941, and Greece was occupied by Nazi forces.

When the Germans withdrew from Greece in 1944, the country's economy was in ruins, and famine was widespread. Communist forces tried to take control of Greece but were defeated in a civil war that ended in 1949. The monarchy returned to power, and the Greek economy received aid from the United States. In 1952 Alexandros Papagos became prime minister. He

Paul I, King of Greece (1947-64), opening the parliament in Oldenburg, Athens on December 12, 1952.

began focusing on the economic reconstruction of the country, and improved international security by joining NATO.

In the 1950s Cyprus, a British colony where the majority of the population was Greek, became the object of a dispute between Greece and Turkey. Britain granted Cyprus independence in 1960, after tense negotiations with Greece, Turkey, and Cyprus.

From 1952 to 1963, an authoritative regime ruled Greece. After a short period of rule by the Center Union Party, a group of military colonels led by George Papadopoulos overthrew the government in 1967. Civil rights were suspended, and the monarchy was abolished. A new constitution was drawn up providing for a stable government but eliminating political freedom.

DEMOCRACY

In June 1973 Papadopoulos proclaimed Greece a republic and announced plans for parliamentary elections. In November of the same year, another group of military officers overthrew the Papadopoulos government.

Andreas Papandreou, prime minister of Greece from 1981-89 and from 1993-96, at a PASOK rally in January 1969.

In 1974 the Greek military tried to overthrow the government of Cyprus. Turkey sent troops to the island, but both countries signed a cease-fire a few days later.

The military government collapsed after the failed takeover of Cyprus amid growing economic problems. Constantine Karamanlis, a former prime minister, was called to head the new government in 1974. Parliamentary elections were held that November, followed by a referendum to make the country a republic.

From 1981 to 1989 the Panhellenic Socialist Movement (PASOK) controlled parliament with Andreas Papandreou as prime minister. In 1990 the New Democratic Party came to power but was defeated by PASOK in the 1992 election. Papandreou became prime minister once again but retired in 1996. Costas Simitis succeeded Papandreou and was re-elected in April 2001. He remained prime minister until March 2004, when he was replaced by Kostas Karamanlis, who was replaced by George Papandreou in October 2009.

Upon inauguration in 2009, Papandreou's government revealed that the country's finances were far worse than previous announcements had indicated, with a budget deficit of 12.7 percent of GDP, four times more than the eurozone's limit, and a public debt of $410 billion. This announcement only served to worsen the already severe crisis the Greek economy was undergoing, with an unemployment rate of 10 percent. After nationwide protests and demonstrations against his government's austerity measures and widespread polls showing the Greek public's disapproval of him as prime minister, Papandreou resigned in November 2011.

Anti-austerity protesters shout slogans and hold a banner reading "1940-NO Andreas Papandreou: Greece belong to Greeks, George Papandreou: Greece belongs to Germans, Merkel=Hitler" during a student parade in Athens on October 28, 2011.

On May 2, 2010, the eurozone countries and the International Monetary Fund (IMF) agreed on a €110 billion loan for Greece, conditional on the implementation of harsh austerity measures. In October 2011 eurozone leaders also agreed on a proposal to write off 50 percent of the Greek debt owed to private creditors. There were widespread fears that a Greek default on its debt would have global repercussions, endangering the economies of many other countries in the European Union, threatening the stability of the euro, and possibly plunging the world into another recession. It has been speculated that the crisis will force Greece to abandon the euro and bring back its former currency, the drachma.

On May 6, 2012, Greece held elections hoping to gain support for the unpopular austerity measures. In a shocking move, voters punished the ruling party that had implemented the austerity measures and swung to far-right, radical parties. Greece held another round of elections on June 17, 2012. The New Democractic Party (ND) won the most seats and currently makes up 30 percent of the government. As of 2013, Antonis Samaras, the ND leader, was serving as the Prime Minister and formed a coalition with PASOK.

INTERNET LINKS

www.bbc.co.uk/schools/primaryhistory/ancient_greeks/

This charming website on ancient Greek history has lovely illustrations and a Greek-hero game.

www.ahistoryofgreece.com/

This is a comprehensive website on the history of Greece from Hellenistic times to the present day, complete with delightful pictures.

http://eudocs.lib.byu.edu/index.php/History_of_Greece:_Primary_Documents

This is a compilation of online primary documents relating to the history of Greece with sources from the British Museum as well as documents of World Wars I and II.

GOVERNMENT

Constructed in 1843, the Hellenic Parliament Building in Athens was originally the palace of Kings Otto and George I. In November 1929, after lengthy debate in Parliament, the government of Eleftherios Venizelos decided to relocate the two chambers of Parliament here. It has been modernized and modified over the years and houses the Greek parliament today.

3

GREECE HAS BEEN A parliamentary republic since 1974. In that year, a new constitution was put into effect, providing for civil liberties and individual rights, which had been abolished during the years of military and authoritative regime. The constitution was amended in 2001.

ADMINISTRATIVE STRUCTURE

According to the Greek constitution, the president is the head of state and the supreme commander of the armed forces. Unlike in the United States, the president is not elected by the people; the Greek parliament appoints the president for a five-year term. Since the president is selected by the political majority in parliament, the president is unlikely to challenge any decisions made by the parliament members; his powers are mainly ceremonial. With the consent of the parliament, however, the president may declare war and sign international agreements concerning peace, alliances, and participation in international organizations. The president may serve a maximum of two terms.

The Hellenic (Greek) Parliament, or *Vouli ton Ellinon*, is the supreme democratic institution that represents the citizens through an elected body of Members of Parliament (MPs). It consists of 300 members, or deputies, who hold office for four years. Members of parliament are elected by the people. The head of the majority political party in parliament is appointed prime minister. Political power lies in the hands of the prime minister.

The Greek Supreme Court handles criminal and civil cases. The Supreme Special Court is the highest court of law in Greece; it deals with constitutional issues and ensures that parliamentary elections are valid. The president, in consultation with a judicial council, appoints its members.

Greek citizens 18 years old and above are required by law to vote in all elections. Voting is done through the secret ballot.

PARLIAMENT AND THE MONARCHY

Constantine II, King of Greece, from 1964 to 1974, with his mother Frederika in an open car in 1967.

The birthplace of democracy, Greece has also experienced undemocratic governments in the course of its history. It is sometimes said that the Greek civilization has been around for so long that it has had a chance to try nearly every form of government.

In the 19th century, during the fight for independence from Turkish rule, many Greeks joined political parties. Each party embraced a different political ideology, so the formation of a new and independent government would not have united these factions. Britain, France, and Russia therefore decided that the best way to avoid political turmoil in Greece was to make the country a monarchy and establish a foreigner as king. Thus the Greek monarchy was born.

Although the Greeks did not object to their foreign king in the beginning, they later questioned the role of the monarchy. In 1844, attempts to curb the absolute power of the king led to the adoption of a constitution that established a legislature. By 1862 discontent led to a second revolt, and King Otto was deposed. The new liberal and democratic constitution of 1864 established a new monarchy under King George I. The constitution called for the creation of a unicameral (one-house) legislature based on representation by vote and very limited powers for the king. Parliament later evolved to a two-house body before reverting to a one-house legislature in 1952.

The issue of whether Greece should continue to have a monarchy was finally resolved in the constitution of 1975, when the monarchy was abolished. King Constantine II was Greece's last king.

DICTATORSHIP AND DEMOCRACY

After the defeat of the communists in 1949, a right-wing government ruled Greece from 1952 to 1963. That government retained its power by repressing political freedom and persecuting its opponents. The population soon grew discontented with the authoritative regime and sought political reform.

In 1964 the Center Union Party, headed by George Papandreou, won the parliamentary elections and came to power. Although Papandreou tried to bring social reform to Greece, his rule did not succeed in putting a stop to the years of riots, strikes, and political fighting. The military stepped in to take full control in April 1967.

The military dictatorship lasted until 1974, when its attempt to overthrow the government of Cyprus met with defeat. The ruling military junta lost the support of senior military officers, who called for Konstantinos Karamanlis, a former prime minister, to return from exile. A new constitution came into effect in June 1975 and established a republic.

Evzones, or Evzoni, marching in Greece.
Though these Presidential guards are predominantly ceremonial, all Evzones are drawn from the Greek Hellenic army's infantry, artillery, and armored corps.

ARMED FORCES

Greece is protected by an army, an air force, and a navy. Greek men must serve nine months in any branch of the armed forces. The government spends about 3.2 percent of the annual GDP on the military, twice as much as any other European Union member on defense.

Until the late 1990s, the greatest threat to Greek security was Turkey, as the two nations have had historical disputes over Cyprus and other territories for decades. The devastating earthquakes that hit both countries in 1999 helped improve relations, with each country coming to the aid of the other.

The island of Cyprus is the third-largest island in the Mediterranean. Cyprus has an area of 3,572 square miles (9,251 square km) and a population of about 800,000.

The Greeks and the Turks are the two main ethnic groups in Cyprus. The Greek-speaking people have lived on the island since the days prior to Alexander the Great. Turkish Cypriots are the descendants of the Ottoman Turks who conquered the island in 1571 and occupied it until 1878, when Britain assumed control of Cyprus. In 1960 Cyprus gained its independence. In 1974 hostilities broke out between the two ethnic groups, and the island was divided. Today, two-thirds of Cyprus is occupied by Greek troops, and the northern one-third is occupied by Turkish forces.

The constitution of Cyprus stipulates that the vice president of the republic and 24 of the 80 members of the House of Representatives must be Turkish. The two communities are self-governing with regard to education, culture, and religion. All matters pertaining to government fall under the jurisdiction of the joint administration.

Since February 1975, however, the post of vice president and 24 seats in the House of Representatives have been vacant, as Turkish Cypriots formed their own government in 1975. The Turkish Cypriot government is not recognized by the United Nations.

POLITICAL PARTIES

Greece's two main political parties are the Panhellenic Socialist Movement (PASOK) and New Democracy (ND), both founded in 1974. Other parties are the Communist Party of Greece and the Coalition of the Radical Left. Recent years have seen the gradual emergence of a staunchly conservative, populist party, the Popular Orthodox Rally, with a platform based on nationalistic, religious, and immigration issues.

The PASOK government ruled Greece for most of the 1980s and 1990s, except for a brief period of coalition governments and New Democracy rule in the late 1980s and early 1990s. The PASOK government brought about significant social reform in Greece—women acquired equal rights, the voting age was lowered to 18, and civil marriage was legalized.

Political parties in Greece are closely associated with the personality of a strong leader. Andreas Papandreou was PASOK's driving force. He remained a key figure in Greek politics until his death in 1996. In the 2000 election, PASOK won by a narrow margin. Constantine Simitis became prime minister and Constantine Stephanopoulos president. Following a narrow victory in the 2009 elections, then prime minister George Papandreou had promised to revive the country's ailing economy with a €3 billion, or $3.7 billion, stimulus package that did not materialize. On June 20, 2012, Harvard-educated conservative Antonis Samaras was sworn in as Greece's fourth prime minister. His party, New Democracy, has forged a coalition with the Socialists (PASOK) and the smaller Democratic Left.

Greek prime minister Antonis Samaras at a pre-election rally in April, 2012. In 2013, Samaras looked to partner with China to help revive the Greek economy.

INTERNET LINKS

www.historyforkids.org/learn/greeks/government/

This is an easy-to-read page about the various types of governments Greece has experienced, complete with links to explanations of terms and other sources.

http://greece.mrdonn.org/government.html

This is an attractive website for kids with explanations on the origins of democracy and the concept of citizenship. It has fantastic cartoons!

**http://ancienthistory.about.com/od/governmen1/
tp/102309GreekGovernment.htm**

This website explains seven interesting points about ancient Greek governments, with links to other pages.

ECONOMY

The National Bank of Greece (NBG) in Plateia Kozia, Athens. NBG is the oldest and largest commercial banking group in Greece. The group has a particularly strong presence in southeastern Europe and the eastern Mediterranean.

4

I N LATE 2009, THE GOVERNMENT of Prime Minister George Papandreou announced that it had discovered its conservative predecessor had falsified budget figures, concealing a swollen debt that was growing rapidly in the wake of the global economic meltdown.

Greece was quickly frozen out of the bond markets, and in May 2010 it began to rely on an aid package of €110 billion, or $152.6 billion, agreed to by its richer European neighbors.

On February 21, 2012, after more than 13 hours of talks in Brussels, European finance ministers approved a new bailout of €130 billion, or $172 billion, subject to Greece taking immediate steps to put into effect the deep structural changes that they had agreed on.

ROOTS OF CRISIS

The roots of the crisis go back to the strong euro and the rock-bottom interest rates that prevailed for much of the past decade. Greece took advantage of this easy money. Not only did the country's consumers rack up debt, but so did its government, which eventually owed $400 billion in debt. Greece's debt is currently at 165 percent of its GDP.

EU MEMBERSHIP: BLESSING OR CURSE?

For Greece the financial crisis has highlighted the constraints of euro membership. Unable to devalue its currency to regain competitiveness

The Greek economy is on the verge of collapse. During the past decade, Greece went on a debt binge that came crashing to an end in late 2009, provoking a crisis that has decimated the country's economy, unleashed increasing social unrest, and threatened both Europe's economic recovery and the future of the euro.

Protesters in front of the Hellenic Parliament in Athens in 2010. Greek workers and civil servants staged a 24-hour strike to show public discontent with government austerity measures, including a radical pension reform aimed at helping the country solve its huge debt crisis.

and forced by EU fiscal agreements to control spending, it is facing austerity measures even though some experts claim its economy needs extra spending.

REACTION TO BAILOUT AND AUSTERITY MEASURES

Greece's leaders contend that the bailout signed in February 2012 allowed the country to avert economic disaster, but Greeks are reacting badly to the new austerity measures. These measures include a 22 percent cut to the private-sector benchmark minimum wage and an increase in value-added tax (VAT) from 21 to 23 percent. Greece's lenders will have the right to seize the gold reserves in the Bank of Greece under the terms of the new deal, and future bonds issued will be governed by English law and in Luxembourg courts, conditions more favorable to creditors. Many Greeks have begun to feel that the debt write-down and the new loan are aimed at saving the banks more than the country and its citizens.

UNEMPLOYMENT IN GREECE

Unemployment stood at an estimated 27.3 percent in early 2013, and among those ages 15-24, the unemployment rate was 64 percent. Disenfranchised youths have been among those demonstrating in Athens against the austerity measures. Many of them have bachelor's or master's degrees, but due to the crisis they are working bottom-rung jobs such as cleaning or serving tea and coffee—if they are working at all. Many of them have left the country for greener pastures, elsewhere in Europe or overseas, such as Australia. In 2011, doctors and nurses staged walkouts over hospital cuts. Taxi drivers hobbled Greece with strikes for two weeks, protesting at government plans to open up the industry. Their tactics included blocking ports and opening the Acropolis ticket office to let tourists in for free.

GREECE AND THE EUROPEAN UNION

The European Union was formed with the signing of the Treaty on European Union in Maastricht, the Netherlands, in February 1992. The Maastricht Treaty was signed by representatives from Belgium, Denmark, France, Germany, Greece, Ireland, Italy, Luxembourg, the Netherlands, Portugal, Spain, and the United Kingdom.

The treaty was the last step on the road to European integration that began in the 1950s with the formation of the European Economic Community (EEC), also known as the Common Market. Later the EEC was referred to as the European Community (EC).

The EU hopes to boost the economic situation of its member countries by creating a general tariff on imports, thus protecting EU industries from foreign competition. In addition, companies based in the EU are allowed to invest in any member country without trade restrictions. The EU also encourages mobility and social integration among its citizens, as they are allowed to reside and settle in any of the member countries. Issues, such as consumer protection, public health, education, industrial policy, foreign policy, security, and environmental protection are handled by a common EU governing body.

Greece joined the EC in 1981 and was one of the signatories of the Maastricht Treaty. The government of Greece, one of the least developed economies in the union, implemented reform programs in order to shape up the economy for membership in the Economic and Monetary Union (EMU). The programs were successful, and Greece became a member on January 1, 2001. The euro became Greece's official currency on January 1, 2002.

Without the bailout packages given by the EU (totaling €349 billion), the Greek economy would have collapsed a long time ago. However, the austerity measures that the EU is demanding have caused a lot of resentment amongst Greek citizens.

Underscoring these actions is a big rift between ordinary Greeks and the politicians, whom most Greeks now distrust. Greece has the EU's second-worst Corruption Perceptions Index, after Bulgaria, ranking 80th in the world, and the lowest score in both the Index of Economic Freedom and the Global Competitiveness Index, ranking 119th and 90th in the world respectively. Corruption, together with the associated issue of poor standards of tax collection, is widely regarded as both a key cause of the current troubles in the economy and a key hurdle in terms of overcoming the country's debt problem. It is estimated that 20 percent of the population live below the poverty line.

Greece is the world's third-leading producer of olives, which flourish in the country's dry climate. The ancient Greeks believed that the goddess Athena had presented Athens with an olive plant and that its cultivation would make the people prosperous. Olive plantations cover the whole of the Peloponnese and much of Sterea Ellas, Crete, and Thessaly.

Hundreds of types of olive trees are grown in Greece. Some varieties are grown for food, others for producing olive oil. The majority of the olive trees in Greece produce olives for oil. In the spring, farmers prune the olive trees and use the trimmings for fuel. Several weeks later small white flowers appear that transform into the familiar hard green fruit. Later in the season, families go out with long poles to knock down the green olives. Green olives are usually exported. Greeks prefer the ripe black olives available later in the season. The black-olive harvest begins in November. Sheets are spread beneath the trees, and pickers on ladders run their hands over the loaded branches. The ripe fruit falls to the sheets; the unripe olives remain on the branches to mature. Several weeks later, the procedure is repeated, and it continues throughout winter. Olives to be eaten are usually pickled in barrels of brine. Olives grown for their oil are crushed immediately after picking.

TOURISM

Tourism used to be the fastest-growing industry in Greece; it accounted for 15 percent of the country's annual GDP, and it still shows potential for further growth. About 19.3 million tourists visit Greece each year, more than the country's entire population.

Beautiful beaches, plentiful sunshine, and breathtaking islands, in addition to the country's matchless cultural heritage, make Greece a favorite vacation spot. More than 90 percent of the tourists come from elsewhere in Europe. During peak season, from mid-June to the end of August, the tourist industry employs about 17 percent of the entire labor force. This figure decreases sharply during the off-season, from the end of November to the beginning of April, when most of the tourist facilities are unused. However, tourists were cautious about visiting Greece in recent years, given the massive strikes and demonstrations the austerity measures unleashed.

During the past decade, the road systems of Greece were in a state of constant repair. Now, most major highways are new and up to the highest international standards.

AGRICULTURE

Greek agriculture is based on small, family-owned units. The extent of a cooperative-organization manner of farming has remained at comparatively low levels, despite efforts during the past 30 years, mainly under European Union supervision. Greek agriculture employs 528,000 farmers, 12 percent of the total labor force, yet it accounts for only 3.6 percent of the national GDP (about $16 billion annually).

Because of the shortage of arable land (only 20 percent of the total land area), Greece does not produce enough grain to feed its population and must import food from other countries. Nevertheless, Greece is a major exporter of cotton and tobacco to the EU. Greece's agricultural products include wheat, corn, barley, sugar beets, olives, tomatoes, wine, tobacco, potatoes, beef, and dairy products.

Wheat, oats, millet, and barley are native to Greece. Olives, grown mainly for olive oil, and grapes, from which juice and wine are made, are also important crops. Currants are another grape product. In fact, *currant* is derived from the phrase "Corinth grape." Other fruits include apricots, dates, figs, oranges, and peaches.

Livestock are raised in pastures and meadows. Due to the lack of rich pasture, however, Greek livestock are of poor quality. Greece imports most of its meat.

Kolymbithres Beach on the island of Paros. Paros has some of the most beautiful and popular beaches in the Greek islands. Tourists, drawn by the unspoiled beaches, warm and clean water, and rock formations, like to windsurf and kitesurf here.

Greek fisherman in Ithaca. The island of Ithaca is located west of the mainland of Greece in the Ionian Sea, the second smallest inhabited island of the seven Ionian islands. The locals work as stock-breeders, technicians, engineers, fishermen, and in tourism.

Since joining the EU, Greece has received subsidies aimed at improving the agricultural sector. As the rural population moves to the cities to find jobs, however, the economic role of agriculture may continue to decline.

FISHING

With a 2,485-mile (4,000-km) coastline around the mainland, plus an additional 6,835 miles (11,000 km) around the Greek islands, Greece offers excellent conditions for fishery operations. The Greeks have practiced fishing and sponge-diving since ancient times. In present-day Greece, about 15,000 people continue to make a living from fishing. They work either on fishing boats or at canneries and food-processing centers near the ports.

The Aegean Sea is rich in fish. Nearly 250 species of fish and crustaceans are found in Greek waters, including bass, carp, cod, mackerel, perch, red mullet, swordfish, lobster, and shrimp. In recent years, overfishing and inefficient fish-stock conservation have damaged the fishing industry, so Greece must import many fish products.

Sponge-fishing has a long tradition in Greece, particularly on the Dodecanese Islands. As uncontrolled harvesting has depleted the traditional fishing areas, divers sometimes go as far as the North African coast to fish for sponges. While at sea, fishermen tear off the sponges' outer membrane to prevent decay. Final trimming, drying, and grading are done at the port.

A LEADER IN SHIPPING

Shipping is one of Greece's most important industries. It accounts for 6 percent of GDP, employs about 160,000 people (4 percent of the workforce), and represents one-third of the country's trade deficit. Earnings from

shipping amounted to €15.4 billion in 2010, while between 2000 and 2010, Greek shipping contributed €140 billion (half of the country's public debt in 2009 and 3.5 times the receipts from the EU between 2000 and 2013). Greece represents 41.49 percent of all the EU's dead-weight tonnage.

Greece also has a large shipbuilding and ship-refitting industry. Its six shipyards near Piraeus are among the biggest in Europe. With the economic crisis, however, the Chinese have largely taken over Piraeus with an eye to make it a conduit for shipping goods into Europe.

INDUSTRY

Industrialization was given a boost when Greece joined the European Community in 1981. As foreign capital flowed into the country, new factories were set up. Government policies have supported the growth of new industries, such as food processing and the production of telecommunications equipment. The industrial sector was hit by the Greek financial crisis throughout 2009 and 2010, with domestic output decreasing by 5.8 percent and industrial production in general by 13.4 percent. Retail trade decreased by 11.3 percent in 2009. The only sector that did not see a decline in 2009 was administration and services, with a minimal growth of 2.0 percent.

Aerial view of the capital city and port of Pothia, on the island Kalymnos. Kalymnos is widely known as an international sponge-harvesting trade center. Travelers come here to climb, scuba dive, hike, and explore caves.

The port of Piraeus in Athens is the largest in Europe and the third-largest in the world.

Hellenic Petroleum S.A. oil refining industrial installation tanks at Ionia in Thessaloniki. In Greece, this company owns and operates three refineries, in Aspropyrgos, Elefsina, and Thessaloniki. This refinery has a nominal annual refining capacity of 898 million gallons (3.4 million tonnes) of crude oil. The three refineries combined cover 68% of the country's total refining capacity.

Athens and Thessaloníki are the primary industrial centers. Greece's main manufactured products are cement, steel, chemicals, electrical equipment, cigarettes, textiles, clothing, and processed foods. Currently Greece is ranked third in the EU in the production of marble (920,000 metric tons), after Italy and Spain.

A quarter of all Greek companies have gone out of business since 2009, and in 2012 half of all small businesses in the country said they were unable to meet payroll. The suicide rate increased by 40 percent in the first half of 2011. A barter economy has sprung up, as people try to work around a broken financial system.

MINING

Greece has a number of rich mineral resources such as lignite, copper, bauxite, perlite, bentonite, gypsum, and gold. Other minerals found in Greece include chromite, zinc, lead, copper, asbestos, and magnesite. However, the Greek mining industry declined in both volume and value in 2009 as a result of the global economic crisis, producing 63.2 million tons (57.3 million metric tons) of minerals. Following the February 2012 bailout package for Greece, shares of Greek-owned mining companies have surged.

Lignite, or brown coal, is found mainly on the island of Euboea, in the central Peloponnese, and in the Ptolemais Basin in the Pindus Mountains. The country has vast reserves of it, so lignite-based power plants account for most domestic power generation. About 90 percent of mined lignite is used to generate electricity. However, the government wants to increase the share of renewable energy in its power production and reduce its carbon emissions in accordance with EU policies. As a member of the EU, the country is obliged to produce at least 20 percent of its energy through renewable sources, but the country has set itself a target considerably higher than this. As a result, the consumption of coal for power generation is expected to fall in the long term. The Aegean Sea may be a source of offshore petroleum, but Greece and Turkey continue to dispute ownership.

Greece, officially, has 10 million barrels of reserves located in the Prinos and Prinos North fields. In 2010 production was about 2,300 barrels a day. Now, with the nation in crisis, a decision has been made to open exploration to international oil and gas companies. An intensive exploration campaign both in the Aegean and near the Ionian Islands could not only improve the finances of the country but also create much-needed job opportunities. With crude-oil prices in the $90—$100-a-barrel range, the economic potential is promising.

Greece's battered public finances got a minor boost from the European Union on February 16, 2012, when the bloc's executive said it would repay the € 35 million ($46 million) it had wrongly fined Athens for errors in its EU farm payments.

INTERNET LINKS

www.divingheritage.com/greecekern2.htm

This website provides a fascinating discussion and pictures about Greek sponge-diving.

http://topics.nytimes.com/top/news/international/countriesandterritories/greece

This section of *The New York Times* website provides coverage of the Greek debt crisis, from how it affects the economy to how the lives of ordinary citizens are coming apart.

www.telegraph.co.uk/finance/debt-crisis-live/9094900/Debt-crisis-and-Greek-bailout-deal-live.html

In-depth coverage of the debt crisis complete with photos and videos.

ENVIRONMENT

A colony of Naked Man Orchids *(Orchis italica)* in a montane grassland habitat on the Kedros Mountains, central Crete. The Naked Man Orchid flowers in April and its flowers are borne in a dense spike which can vary from pale to dark pink and can grow up to 20 inches (50 cm) in height.

5

GREECE IS A MOUNTAINOUS country nearly surrounded by the sea. About the same size as Alabama, Greece boasts a variety of ecosystems, each supporting unique flora and fauna.

Rugged mountain ranges averaging more than 5,000 feet (1,524 m) in height cover about 70 percent of the total land area of the country, including the islands, making most of Greece's terrain uneven.

Greece's climate, in turn, is a reflection of the ruggedness of its terrain, and though largely Mediterranean, it ranges from semiarid in the southern islands to cold and wet in the northern mountains near the border with Bulgaria.

Differences in terrain and climate have made it possible for many of Greece's plant and animal species to develop in relative isolation. Greece has 6,000 recorded species of plants, some of which are endemic, or present only in Greece, including more than 100 varieties of orchid. Forests of birch, pine, and spruce grow in the cold northern region. Many of these forests have been damaged by uncontrolled goat grazing, felling, and forest fires.

Greece's varied wildlife, one of the richest in Europe, includes 116 mammal species, 18 species of amphibians, 59 species of reptiles, 240 bird species, and 250 species of fish. It is estimated that about half of the endemic mammal species are in danger of becoming extinct. Unique species of sea turtles and monk seals, now found in large colonies only in Greek waters, have decreased dramatically during the past few decades.

Greece is home to the Ambracian Gulf Wetlands Reserve, located in the southwestern area of Epirus. Its rare ecosystem, protected by the international Ramsar Convention on Wetlands, houses the last examples of riverbank woodlands, as well as one of the last colonies of silver pelicans in Europe.

In the years since World War II, because of an increase of industrial activities, motor vehicles, and tourists, Greece's natural environment has been severely threatened. In response, the Greek government has passed many bills and laws to improve the environment. Unfortunately, compared with other European nations, Greece has not been the swiftest in protecting its environment.

ENDANGERED SPECIES

Greece is endowed with a rich and varied marine population, from abundant fish to seals, dolphins, and turtles. During the past few decades, Greece's marine life has declined sharply due to overfishing, uncontrolled tourist activities, water pollution, and deliberate killings by fishermen, who regard seals and dolphins as competitors in the hunt for fish.

A male Milos wall lizard (*Podarcis milensis*) basks on a rock on Milos Island.

The *Monachus monachus*, or monk seal, is part of Greece's natural and cultural heritage. The monk seal is described as basking on Greece's sandy shores by Homer in his epic poem *The Odyssey*. The head of a monk seal was even found carved on a coin dated 500 B.C. Once found in large colonies, there are only 450-500 left in the whole world. Dolphins and turtles in the Mediterranean Sea also face extinction.

Not only are some of Greece's marine creatures in danger of extinction, but its land animals are also increasingly threatened by the damaging effects of pollution and hybridization, or interbreeding. The wild goat of Antimilos, an islet in the southwestern Cyclades, is a rare species unique to that area. This goat has brown fur and a black stripe on its back; it is threatened by hybridization with domesticated goats.

The island of Milos and surrounding islets in the Cyclades have a number of endemic reptiles and amphibians. Milos supports 90 percent of the total population of a unique viper species. A rare brown and black lizard with spots also lives on Milos and other nearby Aegean islands. During the Milos wall lizard's (*Podarcis milensis*) reproductive period, the male becomes strongly colored with blue spots on its sides. Milos also serves as a passageway for birds migrating from Africa to Europe.

The Greek government and the EU have passed legislation to protect the endemic creatures of the Cyclades from the threat of extinction.

AIR POLLUTION

Air pollution is a major environmental problem. The air in Athens is degraded by exhaust from automobiles. In the summer, vehicular traffic is responsible for about 80 percent of the smog in Athens. Diesel-run vehicles, such as taxis, buses, and trucks, are major contributors to air

THE MONK SEAL

The Mediterranean monk seal, or Monachus monachus, is Europe's number-one endangered marine mammal and one of the six most endangered mammals in the world. Once present throughout the Mediterranean, Marmara, and Black Seas, as well as along the Atlantic coast of Africa, monk seals have been reduced to around 500, of which about 250 live in Greek waters.

The ancient Greeks hunted monk seals to obtain products that were essential to their survival, such as fur, oil, meat, and medicines. However, the numbers they hunted were never large enough to threaten the species with extinction. During the time of the Roman Empire and later in the Middle Ages, the population of monk seals was almost depleted due to excessive commercial hunting. The remaining monk seal population retreated from the beaches and rocks to inaccessible caves with underwater entrances. Present-day female monk seals choose caves or other undisturbed places to give birth to pups.

Human activity is the main threat to the survival of the monk seal. Monk seals die when they get caught in fishing nets. Fishermen sometimes deliberately kill the monk seals, which they consider a competitor in the hunt for fish. Pollution caused by ships (oil leaks, runoff, and sewage) and uncontrolled tourism (which leads to the encroachment of human settlement into animal habitats) are destroying the monk seal's natural environment. After the Costa Concordia cruise ship ran aground on January 13, 2012, off Giglio Island in Italy, the monk seal was further endangered by the environmental pollution that caused.

The island complex of Milos-Antimilos-Kimolos-Polyaigos has been set apart by the European Union as a reserve, as monk seal shelters have been identified along the shores and newborn pups have been spotted in the area during the reproductive period. This initiative is part of Natura 2000. Milos and the nearby islands belong to a volcanic alignment called the Aegean Volcanic Arc.

pollution. A series of antipollution measures taken by the city's authorities in the 1990s, combined with a substantial improvement of the city's infrastructure (including the Attiki Odos motorway, the expansion of the Athens Metro, and the new Athens International Airport), considerably alleviated pollution and transformed Athens into a much more functional city. In 2004 Athens hosted the Summer Olympics with great success.

Growing industrial cities such as Thessaloníki and Piraeus are also facing the problem of air pollution due to poor waste-disposal methods.

Once infamous for its smog and traffic jams, Athens cleaned up its act to prepare for the 2004 Summer Olympics. A modern metro and new motorways eased the air pollution and traffic congestion.

WASTE DISPOSAL AND RECYCLING

Waste disposal is a major problem in Greece. In 2000 Greece was ordered by the EU to pay a €4.72 million fine for failing to comply with standards for the proper sanitization of landfill sites. As of 2008, however, there were still more than 1,000 illegal landfill sites in operation and more than 1,000 abandoned sites where waste was disposed. The 37 legal landfill sites served only 50 percent of the population. There are only two sanitary landfills in Greece, on the islands of Zákinthos and Lemnos, where biogas and harmful chemicals are treated before they are released into the atmosphere.

Recycling in Greece is not mandatory, and for many Greeks it is last on their list of priorities. However, in the past few years, steps have been taken by the government and nonprofit nongovernmental organizations (NGOs) to educate Greeks on the importance of recycling.

CONSERVATION EFFORTS

Greek NGOs and environmental groups supported by the EU are alerting local and other European citizens to the plight of the environment in Greece.

Sea turtles are migratory. They feed and reproduce in different areas. Although these areas may be hundreds of miles apart, turtles manage to find them with remarkable ease.

MOM The Hellenic Society for the Study and Protection of the Monk Seal (MOM) was established in 1988 by a group of marine biologists and researchers. The aim of this NGO is to gain knowledge about the monk seal by study and research, and to protect the monk seal by all legal means possible. MOM is funded by

THE LOGGERHEAD SEA TURTLE

Greece is home to the last remaining nesting sites in the Mediterranean for the rare loggerhead sea turtle. Every year Laganas Bay on Zákinthos, an island in the Ionian Sea off the northwestern shore of the Peloponnese, hosts 1,300 nests along 8 miles (13 km) of beach. Loggerhead sea turtles are large but gentle creatures that can weigh up to 350 pounds (159 kg). Some 1,200—2,000 turtles crawl out of the sea to lay their eggs on the soft sand beaches. Although they spend most of their life in the sea, loggerheads nest where they were hatched, and the Caretta caretta have been returning to Laganas for more than 10,000 years.

From the end of May until the end of August, loggerheads from different parts of the Mediterranean return to Zákinthos. The female comes ashore at night to lay about 120 eggs resembling ping-pong balls in the sand, and after covering her 20- to 24-inch-deep (50- to 60-cm-deep) nest, she returns to the sea. The female loggerhead may return 15 days later to dig another nest, repeating this process three or four times in one season.

The eggs must remain undisturbed in the warm sand for about 60 days before they hatch. After the eggs hatch, the hatchlings remain in the nest for several days. From late July until the end of October, the hatchlings start to emerge from their nests. They dig their way out of the nest in a joint effort, usually streaming out at night. The hatchlings then make their way down to the sea. The race from their nest to the sea is crucial to their survival, as predators may be waiting nearby. Although a female sea turtle may lay hundreds of eggs each summer, only a small number of hatchlings will survive to adulthood.

Most female loggerheads return to their nesting beaches after two or three years to repeat the nesting cycle. It is thus crucial to the survival of the loggerhead sea turtle that these nests be protected from pollutants or other disturbances such as human intrusion. In 2001 close to €290 million from the EU and around €118 million from the Greek government funded a full-time staff and management program for the country's first marine park. During the summer the staff, plus a crew of 38 volunteers, patrol the turtle-nesting beaches day and night, counting nests, giving out information to tourists, and keeping people away from the most important nesting areas. They stop hotels and visitors from using beach umbrellas (the poles can plunge into buried nests), prevent access to some beaches at night, and patrol beachfront bars, restaurants, and hotels, making sure they keep the music and lights low. Protecting turtles from the intense tourism development and trying to develop a working relationship with the local community has been a challenge, says the park's director, Kostas Katselidis.

The Samariá Gorge is one of the most impressive gorges in Greece. It starts from an altitude of 4,035 feet (1,230 m) and the widest point is 492 feet (150 m) across.

membership dues and contributions from more than 5,500 supporters. MOM also enjoys the support of the EU and has been a member of the International Union for the Conservation of Nature (IUCN) since 1996.

ARCHELON Greece is home to the last remaining nesting sites in the Mediterranean for the rare loggerhead sea turtle (*Caretta caretta*). The Sea Turtle Protection Society of Greece, or Archelon, is a nonprofit organization founded in 1983. Archelon monitors an average of 2,500 nests a year in the major nesting areas, such as Zákinthos, and runs public awareness and environmental education programs. In 1994 Archelon set up the first Sea Turtle Rescue Center in the Mediterranean, which receives and treats sick and injured turtles from all over Greece.

NATIONAL PARKS AND RESERVES IN GREECE

MOUNT OLYMPUS Mount Olympus is the highest mountain in Greece, located on the border between Thessaly and Macedonia. Mount Olympus has 52 peaks. The highest peak rises to 9,570 feet (2,917 m). In Greek mythology Olympus was regarded as the home of the 12 principal gods. It was believed to have formed itself after the gods defeated the Titans in the Titan War and is the setting of many Greek myths. It is estimated that 10,000 people climb Mount Olympus each year.

ALONNISOS MARINE PARK The National Marine Park of Alonnisos Northern Sporades was founded by presidential decree on May 16, 1992. It was the first of its kind in Greece and is currently the largest protected marine area in Europe—873 square miles (2,261 square km). It is located in the region of the Northern Sporades, in the northern Aegean Sea. This is an important habitat for the monk seal, and various species of dolphins and some whale species are also seen in the region.

SAMARIÁ GORGE   The Samariá Gorge is in the White Mountains' National Park on the island of Crete, part of the World Network of Biosphere Reserves. This park offers protection to more than 450 species of plant and animal, 70 of which are native to Crete. The gorge was created by a small river running between the White Mountains and Mount Volakias. There are a number of other gorges in the White Mountains. Samariá Gorge is 10 miles (16 km) long; the most famous part of the gorge is the stretch known as the Iron Gates, where the sides of the gorge close in to a width of only 9.9 feet (3 m) and soar up to a height of 3,610 feet (1,100 m). The gorge became a national park in 1962, particularly as a refuge for the native *kri-kri* Cretan goat, which is largely restricted to the park and an island just off the shore of Agia Marina.

A rare kri-kri (*Capra aegagrus creticus*), spotted in Samaria Gorge, Samaria National Park, Crete. Only about 2,000 kri-kri are left in the world, all to be found on the Greek islands. They remain at risk of being hunted for their tender meat.

PINDUS NATIONAL PARK   Pindus National Park is in mainland Greece, situated in an isolated mountainous area at the periphery of West Macedonia and Epirus, in the northeastern part of the Pindus Mountains. It was established in 1966 and covers an area of 17,120 acres (6,928 ha). It belongs to the Natura 2000 ecological network of protected areas in the European Union and is one of three places in Greece that hosts a population of bears.

INTERNET LINKS

www.greekorchids.gr/

This enchanting website provides lovely pictures of all the orchids in Greece.

http://greekbirding.blogspot.com/

This is a gorgeous website with beautiful pictures of Greek birds.

www.minenv.gr/4/41/e4100.html

The official website of the government agency looking after the environment in Greece, this includes press releases and articles.

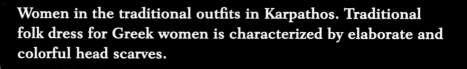

GREEKS

Women in the traditional outfits in Karpathos. Traditional folk dress for Greek women is characterized by elaborate and colorful head scarves.

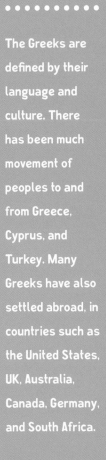

THE POPULATION OF GREECE is nearly homogeneous. According to government statistics, about 93 percent of the people are ethnic Greeks. The remaining 7 percent are Turks, Vlachs, Slavs, Albanians, Jews, and Gypsies.

During the past decade, thousands of immigrants have come to Greece from former communist-bloc countries, such as Albania, in search of work. Ninety-nine percent of Greeks speak Greek with a large part of the population also fluent in English. The population of Greece is 10.8 million (2013 estimate) with 61 percent living in cities.

GREEK PERSONALITY

Traditionally the Greeks have been known for their lack of materialism, search for ideals, respect for the law, and preference for Western European dance and music.

But the Greek personality also has a practical side that focuses on reality, makes decisions on matters concerning money and power, bypasses rules to achieve goals, values education, and loves the country lifestyle and its folk music.

Although some of the traditional stereotypes may be fading, present-day Greeks still place a high premium on family values and maintain close ties with parents, siblings, and the extended family, which may include grandparents, aunts, uncles, cousins, and godparents. Famous for their sense of hospitality, Greeks will often put their guests' needs before their own.

The Greeks are defined by their language and culture. There has been much movement of peoples to and from Greece, Cyprus, and Turkey. Many Greeks have also settled abroad, in countries such as the United States, UK, Australia, Canada, Germany, and South Africa.

POPULATION TRENDS

Greece has a population of 10.8 million (2013 estimate). Most of the population lives on the Greek peninsula; the islands are sparsely populated. The population growth rate in Greece is a low 0.06 percent per year.

After the military junta was overthrown in the mid-1970s, Greeks living in the countryside began migrating to the cities looking for work. As a result, almost half of the present-day population is concentrated in greater Athens and Thessaloníki. Twenty percent of rural Greeks work as farmers in the countryside.

From the late 1800s to the end of World War II, great numbers of Greeks migrated to North America and Australia. Emigration was mainly driven by war, unemployment, and famine. It is estimated that since 1945, 2 million Greeks have moved to Australia and 2 million to the United States.

After Greece joined the EC, Greeks began migrating to Germany and Belgium in search of work. Many, however, have been forced to return to Greece after demand for immigrant labor in these countries declined.

MINORITY GROUPS

During the course of its long history, Greece has been settled by different peoples and empires: Roman, Frankish, Venetian, Byzantine, and Ottoman Turk. Although the present-day population is overwhelmingly ethnic Greek, the ethnic minorities that make up 7 percent of the population are descendants of the early rulers or recent immigrants from Slavic countries.

The minority groups are scattered around the country; some of them have preserved their own language and traditions.

TURKS Most of the Turks in Greece live in Thrace, the northeastern province of Greece along the border with Turkey. Many villages in Thrace have Turkish majorities, and the local governments are run by Muslim officials. The Turkish community in this region numbers 100,000 people.

In 1923, after a Greek invasion to take over Smyrna, a Turkish city with a large ethnic Greek population, led to bloody fighting between the countries,

Greece and Turkey conducted a brutal population exchange. About 400,000 Turks living in Greece were deported to Turkey, and nearly 1.3 million Greeks in Turkey were forced out of their homes and marched to Greece. However, some Turks living in Thrace were able to remain.

Despite ongoing friction between Turkey and Greece, especially over Cyprus, the inhabitants of Thrace live together peacefully. Turkish children attend schools where the language of instruction is Turkish. Several Turkish-language newspapers are also published in Thrace.

Elderly Vlach shepherd in the Zagorian Mountains. A small number of Vlach and Sarakatsani shepherds still practice the *"dhiava,"* an ancient tradition of moving their sheep to higher grazing grounds in the summer.

VLACHS Greek villagers use the word *Vlach* to mean "shepherds." Since the Aromani and Koutsovlach ethnic minorities have traditionally worked as shepherds, they are called Vlachs. The Vlachs, who number 100,000, speak a Romanian dialect and are believed to have come from Romania. They worship in the Greek Orthodox Church.

Another group of shepherds, the Sarakatsani, are often mistaken for Vlachs. The Sarakatsani speak only Greek and have a different set of values and social structure from the Vlachs. Nevertheless, as the groups engage in the same trade, they are in constant competition for grazing land.

ALBANIANS Many Albanians migrated to Greece in the 14th century. Most of them have assimilated into Greek society. Since 1991 a new wave of Albanian immigrants have come to Greece to work, mostly illegally. It is estimated that there are 500,000 recent Albanian immigrants living in Greece today. They have faced difficulties and endured discriminatory treatment by the Greek authorities and the media.

The Turkish community in Thrace makes up 29 percent of the population.

JEWS Jews have lived in Greece since before the time of Christ. In the 13th century, Jewish immigrants from Italy, France, Germany, and Poland settled in Thessaloníki. The greatest influx, however, came in the 15th century, when Sephardic Jews, expelled from Spain during the Inquisition, settled in Greece, where there was religious tolerance under Turkish Muslim rule.

During the Nazi occupation of Greece in World War II, most Jews were taken to concentration camps throughout Europe. The Jewish population in Greece fell sharply from 78,000 to less than 13,000 at the end of the war.

Greek Jews today are mainly merchants or professionals. Thessaloníki is still a center of Jewish intellectual and commercial life, but the majority of Greek Jews live in Athens. The Jewish community in Greece currently amounts to roughly 5,000 people.

SLAVS There are two Slavic groups in Greece: the Slavs from Macedonia and the Pomaks from Thrace. Although they have lived in Greece for centuries, Macedonian Slavs continue to speak Slavic languages. The Bulgarian-speaking Pomaks are Muslims who did not migrate to Turkey in the 1920s. The Slavs in Greece are estimated to number about 200,000.

SOCIAL DIVISIONS

There are no strict class divisions in Greece. Generally Greeks are able to climb up the social ladder through higher education or property ownership.

In villages, the lowest level of society is made up of landless farm laborers. The middle classes are small-farm owners, merchants, and skilled workers. Prosperous farm owners, owners of large shops, successful merchants, professionals, and government officials make up the upper levels.

In towns, the lowest class owns no property and has little education. They are laborers, unskilled factory workers, and domestic servants. The lower middle class consists of craftsmen, owners of small shops, traders, and civil servants. The upper middle class includes professionals, businesspeople, and senior government officials. Urban upper classes include mercantile shipowners, bankers, and industrialists.

FOLK DRESS

Each province in Greece boasts its own traditional clothing. Greeks wear these outfits on special and festive occasions. Although the clothing of each province will reflect a pattern and style from a particular period in Greek history, they generally have one thing in common—the fabric contains exquisite and elaborate embroidery. Greek women have excelled at embroidery for centuries.

Folk dress for women consists of colorful skirts and embroidered vests. An important item in women's folk dress is the colorful scarf worn on the head. Necklaces, earrings, and bracelets add richness to women's dress.

A popular folk outfit for men is the *foustanella* (foos-tah-NEL-lah), a pleated white skirt, which is worn by the evzones, the guards of the presidential residence and the parliament. During ceremonial occasions, they wear a white shirt, a *foustanella*, an embroidered dark-blue jacket, white stockings, and red shoes with pom-poms on the toes. A hat tops the outfit.

Greek Americans participate in the Greek Independence Day Parade in New York City.

INTERNET LINKS

www.greekfolkmusicanddance.com/greekcostume.php

This is a charming page on Greek costumes.

www.greekprideri.com/costume.html

This website showcases all the regional costumes of Greece.

www.gamersenterprise.com/play.php?act=play&id=1273&name=Folk-Fashion-Greece

On this website you can dress up a model in Greek costumes.

LIFESTYLE

A Greek family celebrates over Christmas dinner in Athens. A traditional Christmas dinner consists of roast lamb, pork, or turkey. Loaves of sweet christopsomo ("Christ bread") can usually found on the Christmas table, along with honey-covered biscuits (melomakarana), and kourabiedes (icing sugar-coated biscuits).

7

GREEKS EMBRACE HELLENISM, an ideology based on the ideals that were regarded as exceptional and glorious in ancient Greece. All Greeks, regardless of background, occupation, or region, are aware of the tremendous role their ancestors played in the development of Western civilization.

During the years of Turkish rule, Greeks relied on Hellenism to retain their identity. This ideology lives on today, as modern Greeks strive to follow in their ancestors' footsteps by contributing their knowledge and cultural heritage to global society.

THE FAMILY

A traditional Greek family is usually large, including grandparents and many children, but modern society has affected the structure of the Greek family. Unmarried adults rarely leave their parents' home to live on their own, and in some regions it is the custom for married children to live with their parents until they have established their own households. Greek families are characterized by close-knit relationships, big family feasts for every important occasion, and the presence of a strong matriarchal figure.

Traditionally, a rural newlywed couple lives in the home of the groom's parents or in a home his parents provide for them in the village. If labor is needed for the family farm, married children may continue to

The Hellenistic period (Greek civilization immediately following the ancient Greeks), from 323 B.C. to about 146 B.C., represents the zenith of Greek influence in the world.

Greek family enjoying a forest picnic in Lagadas, a town in Thessaloníki.

live with their parents indefinitely. On some of the islands, a married couple lives in the wife's village, and often her family provides the home as part of the traditional wedding gift.

Family members in Greece work together to maintain the family property. In poorer families with no property, the sons contribute their wages. A Greek considers it a special duty to take care of his or her parents for as long as they live. It is natural for elderly parents to move in with their married children after they have established independent households. As a result, few senior citizens live alone or in homes for the elderly.

SPECIAL RELATIONSHIPS

KOUMBAROS/KOUMBARA In Greece a special bond exists between some families that are not related. This relationship is based on the tradition of choosing a *koumbaros* (koom-BAH-rohs) or a *koumbara* (koom-BAH-rah), a family friend who acts as the best man or the maid of honor at a wedding. Often he or she will also be asked to be the godparent of the couple's first child. As such, the *koumbaros* or the *koumbara* becomes a spiritual member of the family.

Although it is an artificially created kinship, religious law prohibits marriage between the children and the godchildren of a *koumbaros*, because the relationship between the family and the *koumbaros* is considered as close as that of blood relations.

PATRIDA A Greek's homeland is his or her *patrida* (pah-TREE-dah). During the past 200 years, millions of Greeks left their country to start new lives in faraway countries such as the United States and Australia. However, Greeks remain extremely devoted to their homeland. It is not unusual for Greeks living overseas to show their patriotism by flying the Greek flag on their homes and businesses on Greek Independence Day.

PATRONAGE Greeks are intensely loyal to people in the family but traditionally distrustful of people who are not their relatives. In addition, a long history of unstable governments has led Greeks to feel that the only people they can truly rely on are family members. Government and public officials, in general, are regarded with hostility.

This widespread belief has created a heavy reliance on patrons, people of high political standing who look after others in exchange for allegiance. This give-and-take relationship serves both the patron and the benefactor and often lasts a lifetime. For example, besides pledging political support, a fisherman may offer a weekly gift of fish to the patron in return for speeding up a bureaucratic procedure.

PHILOXENIA Hospitality, or *philoxenia* (fee-loh-xeh-NEE-ah), is an old Greek tradition. Some say it began in Homeric times as a sacred duty; others feel that the harshness of the Greek landscape may have caused Greeks to be kind to anyone in need of food or shelter.

Whatever its origin, it is clear that strangers benefit from the consideration that Greeks have for the wants and needs of others. Greeks judge themselves by the extent of their hospitality. If they fail in their duty to put their guests' needs before their own, they will have damaged the honor of not only their ancestors but also of the community as a whole.

This ancient Greek institution of *philoxenia* was spread around the ancient world through the cultural exchange that occurred during travels, trade, and conquest. Throughout the centuries Greeks often found themselves in foreign places, with a need for lodging, help, or protection. *Philoxenia*, therefore, enabled them to find what they needed.

This treatment of strangers began from the belief that the gods themselves, transformed in human form, visited people to check who kept the religious rules and obeyed the laws.

GREEK WOMEN

In the rural areas and villages of Greece, men and women still hold traditional roles. Marriage and family make up the main focus of life for Greek women, and many in the older generation measure their worth by their accomplishments as mothers and homemakers. The men are expected by society to be responsible for providing food and shelter for the family. The house is such an important factor in the life of a Greek woman that people often compare the cleanliness of the living space to the character of the woman who inhabits it.

In the cities, the traditional attitude about the role of the sexes is less evident than in the rural areas. Traditional beliefs about these roles have increasingly been eroded by urbanization. More women are entering the workforce and earning their own living. As a result, women have a greater sense of independence. The double-income family, where both marriage partners work and contribute to household expenses, is also becoming increasingly common in Greece today.

Many of the gains made by Greek women were achieved only in the years after World War II. Women first won equal voting rights in 1952. The following year, the first women were elected to Greece's parliament. By 1977, women made up 38.7 percent of all university students in Greece; by 1980, 9.5 percent of the country's army and 5 percent of the navy consisted of women. By 2000, women made up 40 percent of the Greek workforce and 60 percent of university graduates. Regardless of the fact that women enjoy equal rights with men before the law, however, women on average earn only about 80 percent of a man's wages for performing the same job.

The year 1983 was significant for women's rights in Greece. The country's Family Law came into force, making the spouses equal in decision making. It gave women the right to keep their birth names after marriage; legalized divorce by mutual consent; and abolished a married woman's need to get her husband's permission to conduct business, remove her children from the city, or put them in a school.

Melina Mercouri (1925-94) in Vienna with her husband, American director, screenwriter and actor Jules Dassin, in the 1950s, they collaborated on many movies together.

In 1981 film actress Melina Mercouri became the country's first woman Minister of Culture, a post she was to hold for eight years. She fought for the British to return the Parthenon Marbles, carvings and statues that were taken from the country and shipped to Britain in the early 19th century.

In 1992, at the summer Olympic Games in Barcelona, Paraskevi Patoulidou won the 100-meter hurdles, becoming the first Greek track-and-field medalist since the modern Olympics began in 1896. Ekaterini Thanou followed in her footsteps by securing a silver medal in the same category at the 2000 Olympic Games in Sydney. Former member of parliament Dora Bakoyiannis, a member of the New Democracy Party, became the first woman mayor of Athens when she won the municipal elections held in October 2002. Obviously, the days when Greek dramatist Euripides wrote "a woman should be everything in the house and nothing outside it" are long past!

During World War II, in places such as the Greek island of Crete, the locals, urged on by their *philotimo*, would risk their lives to hide and shelter Australian and British soldiers from the Nazi German occupying forces.

PHILOTIMO

Philotimo (fee-LOH-tee-moh) is a word that describes the feeling of honor that is ingrained in the daily behavior of many Greeks. *Philotimo* involves gaining the respect of others for oneself and one's family by upholding the family honor. Young children in Greece are taught from an early age to avoid losing face in public, as it would be a disgrace to the family honor.

Philotimo is important at all levels of society. Family honor is so sacred that, until recently, a typical defense in many murder cases was that the crime had been committed to uphold the family honor.

EDUCATION

Greeks value formal education greatly, as it is considered an essential requirement for improving one's status in society.

The Greek education system has undergone reform in the past 30 years to become more accessible to all members of society and to offer more practical courses. As a result, the literacy rate has risen from just 30 percent in the 1950s to 97.6 percent today.

A village school room in Crete.

Public education in Greece is compulsory and free. All children aged 6 to 12 must attend *dimotiko* (dee-moh-tee-KOH), or elementary school. Three years of *gymnasio* (gee-MNAH-see-oh), or middle school, follows *dimotiko*. *Lyceum* (LIE-ce-um), or high school, is not mandatory, but most students do attend, graduating after three years. After high school, students take examinations to enter a university or a technical school.

SCHOOL ELECTIONS

Greece is the birthplace of democracy, so it is not surprising that every Greek is introduced to democracy at an early age. From the fifth year of primary school to the third year of *lyceum*, elections are held every September, divided into two parts. In the first part every student elects the *presidium* (ruling body) of his or her class. The class *presidium* has five members: the president, the general secretary, the treasurer, the first member, and the second member.

In the second part students elect a school council, which consists of 15 members, including the school president, the vice president, and the treasurer. Its role is extremely important in every school because the school council makes significant decisions for all the students.

FRIENDS

Greeks love to socialize and spend time with friends. During warm-weather months, families go out every night, and many take long walks on Sunday afternoons. Greeks also love to talk—they love poetry, arguing about politics, and wordplay. They would rather pass time at a crowded beach or park than take a short trip to get some peace and quiet.

After an evening jaunt, elderly men often stop at the local *kafeneío* (kah-fay-NEE-o), or café. A traditional *kafeneío* is patronized almost exclusively by men. Greek men enjoy discussing world events with their friends over a cup of coffee or a glass of wine. Political alliances also play a part in the life of a *kafeneío*, as supporters of a particular political party may gather at one *kafeneío*, while supporters of a rival party gather at another. The younger generation, however, prefer outdoor recreation, clubbing, and dancing.

LOVE IS IN THE AIR

In traditional Greek society, single people did not choose whom they would marry; this was arranged by the parents of the young couple.

Such matrimonial matchmaking is increasingly rare in modern society, especially in the cities. Nevertheless, parental approval is still very important to young people, and few will go against their parents' wishes should they voice strong objections to a prospective partner.

Until the 1960s, young unmarried women in Greece dressed and behaved very modestly. A young woman's demure appearance was regarded as a

Friends exchanging greeetings in a mountain village in Crete.

A Greek Orthodox wedding ceremony.

symbol of the family honor. Women could not spend time alone with a man until they were formally engaged, as any hint of flirtation on the woman's part could damage her reputation and the family honor.

Present-day Greek women living in the cities, however, dress in the latest fashions from Western Europe and North America, which do not always conform to the traditional principles. Young men and women might meet while traveling, through the Internet, at the beach, or at clubs.

TYING THE KNOT

Civil marriages have been legal since 1982, but most Greek couples regard a church ceremony as the only valid contract. Traditionally, the wedding ceremony in a Greek Orthodox church symbolizes the formation of the family. Although the Greek Orthodox wedding ceremony does not include the exchange of vows, it is nevertheless filled with rites that symbolize the unity of husband and wife in a sacred bond.

Nowadays, young couples prefer to have only one or two children; and with most women pursuing a career, household chores and responsibilities are increasingly being shared by the couple. Traditionally seen as an affront to the family honor, divorces in Greece have increased dramatically since the 1960s. The divorce rate in Greece is now 24 percent.

The dowry was an honored tradition in Greek marriages. Women used to enter marriage with a sum of money or a piece of property given to the couple by her parents. The dowry was meant to help the young couple establish their first home, but it also gave the parents some authority over the decisions made by the newly wed couple.

The dowry is now illegal and young urban Greek couples prefer to live apart from their parents.

CHILDREN

Women make up 52 percent of the Greek population. About 40 percent of the workforce consists of women.

Greeks love children, often seeing them as a necessary fulfillment of marriage. In traditional society, *philotimo* is associated with having children.

Traditionally, manhood depended, in part, on the ability to produce a son, although having a daughter was considered better than remaining childless. For the woman, the ideal was to become a mother and educate her children to uphold the family and community values.

The birth of a child is a major event, especially if it is the first child. The rites leading to adulthood begin with baptism. A child receives his or her religious and regional identity when his or her name is pronounced in the presence of the priest, godparents, and parents.

A chrisma (CHRIS-mah), or confirmation ceremony, follows the baptism. The child's forehead, eyes, hands, and feet are anointed with special myrrh from the Patriarchate of Constantinople, thus marking his or her official membership into the Greek Orthodox Church.

In the first four years of life, Greek children are indulged by both parents. By age six, however, Greek children are considered responsible family members who also contribute to keeping the family honor. As they grow up,

Baptism in a church on the island of Sikinos.

they become more aware of philotimo to ensure that they will have the respect of others. Greek parents also pay a lot of attention to the development of their children's language abilities.

DEATH RITUALS

Death rituals in Greece are marked by mourners in black during funerals and memorial services. After the church service, a procession of family and friends makes its way along the streets to the cemetery, where a shorter service is held before the internment of the coffin. The dead are always buried, as the Greek Orthodox Church forbids cremation.

The most important memorial services take place 40 days after death and again on the fifth anniversary of the death. A standard part of the fifth-year memorial is to exhume the body and remove the bones. The bones are first washed with wine, then placed in an ossuary, a depository for the bones of the dead.

Rituals that mark transitions from one stage of life to another are considered by Greeks to be similar in nature. For example, mourning songs and wedding songs are much the same, and it is common for young unmarried people to be buried in white clothes.

Greek family enjoying a meal out at a restaurant on the tiny sandy beach of Sklethri.

WORRY BEADS

A traditional pastime for Greek men in a kafeneío is to click away at their worry beads. The beads range from plastic to silver to mother-of-pearl and are strung on thread and held in the hand. The clicking sound that is made as the fingers "count" the beads creates a type of background music that accompanies lively conversations in many kafeneíos.

Greek men have been using these beads for centuries. Contrary to their name, worry beads, or komboloi (kohm-boh-LOY), have little to do with worry. In fact, the use of these beads is said to be the oldest and simplest way to relieve stress.

Worry beads may have been first used in India by Hindus and Buddhists as prayer beads. Later, Muslims also began using them as prayer beads, often with 99 beads per string to honor the number of ways Allah is glorified. The Greeks may have adopted the use of worry beads from the Turks, who are Muslim.

Roman Catholics also have a tradition of using rosary beads to count prayers. In Greece, however, the use of these beads never achieved any religious significance; rather it evolved into a secular pastime practiced by older men.

INTERNET LINKS

www.worldlyweddings.com/greek-traditions-a/126.htm

This web page contains lovely photos and descriptions of Greek wedding traditions.

http://greece.mrdonn.org/education.html

This is a fascinating page on education in ancient Greece.

www.ancient-greece.us/women.html

This is an interesting page on the role of women in ancient Greece and the contrast between Athenian and Spartan women.

RELIGION

The colorful interiors of the Church of the Tessaron Martiron (Four Martyrs) in Rethymno, Crete.

THE OFFICIAL RELIGION of Greece is Greek Orthodox Christianity, an autonomous faction of the Eastern Orthodox Church. While there is tolerance for other religions, the constitution refers to Greek Orthodox Christianity as the official religion.

The majority of Greeks, about 98 percent, are members of the Greek Orthodox Church. The Orthodox Church has about 150 million members worldwide, of whom 10 million are within Greece. Of the remaining 2 percent of the Greek population, 1.3 percent are Muslim, and 0.7 percent are Jewish, Protestant, or Roman Catholic.

CHRISTIAN BEGINNINGS

Christianity was brought to Greece at the beginning of the first century by the apostle Paul. But it was not until A.D. 313, when Emperor Constantine was converted after seeing a vision of a cross in the sky, that Christianity became the official religion of the Roman Empire.

Constantine moved the capital from Rome to Byzantium, later renamed Constantinople, in present-day Turkey. Geographical, cultural, and linguistic differences between the two capitals led to a bitter rivalry between the bishop of Constantinople, called the patriarch, and the pope in Rome.

Both sides disagreed sharply on who had final authority over matters of faith. The pope insisted that he had absolute power over the entire church, while the patriarch held firm that decisions on matters of faith

8

Religion is, for historical reasons, considered to be part of Greek culture. The Greeks' firm religious beliefs are reflected in the altars and facades of many Greek homes.

must be made by a council. They also disagreed on the issue of celibacy for priests. In 1054 the patriarch and the pope excommunicated one another, marking the division of the Christian church. From that time on, the patriarch of Constantinople represented the Eastern Orthodox Church, and the pope headed the Roman Catholic Church.

CHURCH AUTHORITIES

Eastern Orthodox Church beliefs and practices have remained unchanged since the first millennium. *Orthodox*, in fact, is derived from a Greek word that means "correct belief," emphasizing that the religion is devoted to the original faith of the first apostles.

After Greece became independent from the Ottoman Empire, the Greek Orthodox Church gained independence from Eastern Orthodox patriarchal authority. The Greek Orthodox Church is currently governed by the Holy Synod, a body consisting of all Greek Orthodox bishops. The synod meets once a year under the chairmanship of the archbishop of Athens and All Greece to discuss matters concerning the church.

Bishops in the annual festival procession at St. Gerasimos Monastery on the Greek Mediterranean island of Kefalonia.

The Greek Orthodox Church has no figure comparable to the pope. The ecumenical patriarch of Istanbul, formerly known as the patriarch of Constantinople, is the patriarch and spiritual leader of all the Orthodox churches. Unlike the pope, however, he is not considered infallible, as ancient Christian belief emphasized the equality of all bishops.

RELIGIOUS PRACTICES

For centuries, religion has been closely associated with Greek nationalism. During the years of Turkish rule, the church was the one institution that united all Greeks. The patriarch of Constantinople maintained both spiritual and civil powers over the Greek population, while monks and village priests held secret classes to preserve the Greek language and the Orthodox faith among Greeks. Churches soon became sanctuaries dedicated to the preservation of Greek culture and faith.

Although most of the Greek population is affiliated with the Orthodox Church, and all the important ceremonies in a Greek's life, such as baptism, marriage, and the funeral, are held in church, many Greeks do not attend church regularly. However, their faith is evident in their day-to-day activities.

Greek Orthodox priest pours olive oil into a grave. The Greeks regard olive oil to be as precious as "liquid gold" and have a custom of breaking small containers of olive oil at funerals.

Today Greeks commonly refer to Mount Athos as the Holy Mountain.

Ancient peoples throughout the world have tried to make sense of the natural world by attributing natural phenomena, such as rain, thunder, and earthquakes, to the work of gods and goddesses. Scandinavian, Chinese, Indian, and Egyptian mythologies have gods whose exploits reflect the character of the people. The Greeks also had their own pantheon of gods, and the colorful stories created around them have influenced European thought and culture since ancient times. Many stories or myths about the Greek gods originated as early as 700 B.C.

Myths of the gods were passed down from generation to generation through storytelling and poetry and have been preserved through the ages in the works of the classical Greek writers. Homer's The Iliad *and* The Odyssey *and Hesiod's* Theogony *incorporate most of the characters and themes of classical Greek mythology.*

Theogony *describes the origin and history of the gods. According to this work, the universe was formed from an empty and shapeless mass called Chaos. From Chaos sprang Gaea, or Earth, who gave birth to Uranus, or Heaven. Gaea and Uranus, as rulers of the universe, gave birth to the Titans. The Titan Atlas (below) held up the celestial sphere and two Titans, Cronus and Rhea, had six children. These children became the Olympian gods Demeter, Hades, Hera, Hestia, Poseidon, and Zeus. Other Olympian gods included Aphrodite, Apollo, Ares, Artemis, Athena, Hermes, and Hephaestus.*

The Olympian gods were thought to dwell in the sky or on Mount Olympus in Thessaly, which is how they got their name. Earthbound gods were believed to live on or under the earth. Leading the ranks of gods was Zeus, the father of the gods. Hera, his wife, was the queen of the heavens and the goddess of marriage. Among Zeus's brothers and sisters were Poseidon, god of the sea, and Hestia, goddess of hearth and home.

Zeus (right) *had many children who were also gods. Hephaestus was the god of fire; Athena was the goddess of wisdom; Apollo was the god of the sun, music, and poetry; Artemis was the goddess of wildlife and the moon; Ares was the god of war; Aphrodite was the goddess of love; Hermes was the gods' messenger to humans and later god of science and invention; and Dionysus was the god of wine and drama.*

Because each god or goddess ruled over some part of the world and the lives of humans, ancient Greeks worshipped those who could influence their everyday needs. For example, Poseidon, god of the waters, could oversee a successful voyage; Athena, with her wisdom, could help a person solve a problem.

There were also lesser beings, such as the nymphs, who guarded nature, and the Fates, who controlled the destiny of all humans. In addition there were nine Muses, goddesses who provided inspiration for the arts and sciences. Calliope was the Muse of epic poetry; Clio, the Muse of history; Erato, the Muse of lyric poetry; Euterpe, the Muse of music; Melpomene, the Muse of tragedy; Polymnia, the Muse of sacred poetry; Terpsichore, the Muse of dance and song; Thalia, the Muse of comedy; and Urania, the Muse of astronomy.

Roman mythology is nearly identical to that of the Greeks. The Romans greatly admired Greek civilization, so they adopted many Greek gods as their own and gave them Roman names: Zeus was called Jupiter; Poseidon was called Neptune; Dionysus was called Bacchus; Aphrodite was called Venus; and Hermes was called Mercury.

Most Greek families devote a corner of their home to a display of icons and religious paintings, along with lamps and holy oil. In times of trouble, Greeks sometimes go to church to seek divine intervention by lighting and placing a candle at the foot of the image of a famous saint.

The most important festivals in the Greek calendar are based on Christian events, such as Easter and Epiphany. Even secular events such as the harvest or the return of a fishing fleet from the sea are celebrated by small religious ceremonies. Priests may also be asked to bless the opening of a new shop or the building of a house. Patron saints' days are more important celebrations than birthdays.

Religion is a strong unifying factor in the countryside. Local churches are often the focus of a community, and all projects concerning the church are a means of drawing villagers together to work for a common cause.

Mount Athos is a UNESCO World Heritage Site. It is a self-governing part of the Greek State, administrated by the Ecumenical Patriarch of Constantinople. Mount Athos consists of 20 Orthodox monasteries and only men are allowed to enter.

WEARING THE ROBES

In contrast to the Roman Catholic clergy, Eastern Orthodox priests can be married, provided that they are married before ordination. Once a man has been ordained, he may not marry. If a married priest becomes a widower, he is not allowed to remarry. Only unmarried and celibate priests are eligible to become bishops; married priests cannot become bishops.

Since married priests cannot rise to higher office, married men who decide to become priests receive only two years of theological training rather than higher religious education.

Although Christianity replaced the pagan faiths of the Greeks some 1,700 years ago, remnants of the ancient beliefs have survived. Many of these superstitions do not follow the teachings of the church. Crucifixes and charms in the form of eyes are believed to ward off the "evil eye," bad luck that is the result of other people's jealous stares.

Instead of medical doctors, magic healers are sometimes called upon to treat the sick. It is estimated that there are more than 15,000 professional astrologers and fortune-tellers in Greece.

Sacrificial animal offerings still take place. In Gouménissa, a village near Thessaloníki, the tradition of sacrificing a calf continues yearly at a wayside chapel, and the occasion is celebrated with folk dancing and feasting.

***THE** ANASTENARIA is a ritual of fire-walking and spirit possession that takes place in the Macedonian villages of Agia Eleni and Langadhás (below). These rites are performed by Kostilides, a group of people from eastern Thrace who settled in Macedonia in the 1920s. The rites, however, may have started as early as 1250, when a group of Thracian villagers rescued icons from a burning church.*

The Anastenaria begins on May 21, when the Greek Orthodox Church celebrates the festivals of Saint Constantine and his mother, Saint Helen (Eleni). Dancers hold onto icons of these two saints as they make their way across burning coals. Saint Constantine is believed to possess the fire-walking dancers and protect them from harm as they step on the hot coals. At the beginning, the dance is one of suffering, but it transforms into one of joy.

Anastenaria fire-walkers claim to feel warmth but no pain. After leaving the fire, the participants feel they have acted according to the will of the saint. Before the fire dance, a calf is sacrificed. The celebration lasts through May 23.

Anastenaria rites are not recognized by the Greek Orthodox Church, which regards the dancers as heathens. Fire-walkers have been excommunicated by the church.

The Holy
Monastery of
Rousanou, one
of the twenty-
four medieval
monasteries called
Meteora on top
of the Pindus
Mountains. Long
ago, monks
used to scale
the sheer cliffs
in hanging
baskets or
by climbing
rope ladders.

Rural priests are often men of little schooling who receive small salaries from the government. To support their families, rural priests usually must also farm or work the land, just like the other villagers. Although he is respected for his special duties and obligations, the villagers do not hold the local priest in awe. Rural priests are regarded as family men who must provide for their families in the same way as other village men.

Greek Orthodox clergymen wear flowing black robes and black rimless hats. For the church service, colorful brocade vestments are added. Traditionally the clergy did not shave or cut their hair, which was tied in a coiled knot at the base of their neck.

MONASTIC LIFE

Monasteries play an important role in the Greek Orthodox Church. Even before the arrival of Christianity in Greece, Greeks went to monasteries to practice spiritual discipline, spending the day in prayer and meditation. Unlike their counterparts in the Roman Catholic Church, Orthodox monks are often laymen, which means they are not part of the clergy.

Mount Athos, near Thessaloníki, is famous for its many monasteries, some dating back to the 10th century. This religious haven has been granted semiautonomous status from Greece. Only men are allowed to visit the area.

Throughout the history of Greek monasteries, the numbers of monks has fluctuated. Surprisingly, in the past 30 years there has been a resurgence in interest among young men in leading a spiritual life. More than 1,000 monks currently live on historic Mount Athos.

There are three types of Greek Orthodox monks. The cenobitic monks live in a community and share meals, property, services, and work. Idiorrhythmic monks withdraw in small settlements, often in the desert, and pray according to their own schedule, coming together with other monks only on feast days and Sundays. Anchorites were people who were usually walled into a small cell that was attached, or anchored, to a church or an oratory. The difference between a hermit and an anchorite was that a hermit sought solitude and also lived in a small cell but was generally free to come and go. Hermits could farm or hunt for themselves, while anchorites were wholly dependent on others to feed them.

Greece's monasteries are located in remote places, such as the Pindus Mountains of Thessaly.

INTERNET LINKS

www.macedonian-heritage.gr/Athos/General/Introduction.html

This website contains a concise write-up on Mount Athos, the oldest monastic republic still in existence today, together with a description of the three types of Greek Orthodox monks.

www.historyfish.net/anchorites/what_are_anchorites.html

This is a fascinating page on anchorites and the solitary movement with interesting pictures.

www.greekmythology.com/Books/Hesiod-Theogony/hesiod-theogony.html

The entire translation of Hesiod's *Theogony*, broken down into sections, is provided in this website.

LANGUAGE

Elderly Greek women in traditional clothing meet in the small northern mountain town of Metsovo.

9

GREEK, THE OFFICIAL LANGUAGE of Greece, has been spoken for more than 3,000 years, making it the oldest language in Europe. When other European societies had not yet developed a written language, the Greeks were cultivating a rich literary tradition.

Greece is linguistically homogeneous, as most of the population speaks Greek. Minority groups in Greece, which account for 2 percent of the population, speak their own languages—a Romanian dialect called Vlach, Turkish, Slav, Albanian, or the Bulgarian dialect Pomak—in addition to Greek.

A typical book store in Greece.

Greek roots are often used to coin words in other languages, especially in the sciences and medicine; Greek and Latin are the predominant sources of the international scientific vocabulary. More than 50,000 English words are derived from the Greek language.

A α	*alpha*	*a as in father, arm*
B b	*beta*	*v as in violent*
G g	*gamma*	*g as in guild*
D d	*delta*	*d as in democracy*
E e	*epsilon*	*e as in get*
Z z	*zeta*	*z as in zoo*
H h	*eta*	*ee as in meet*
U u	*theta*	*th as in theater*
I i	*iota*	*i as in police*
K k	*kappa*	*k as in kitten*
L l	*lamda*	*l as in lion*
M m	*mi*	*m as in miss*
N n	*ni*	*n as in nose*
J j	*xi*	*x as in fix*
O o	*omicron*	*o as in hot*
P p	*pi*	*p as in 'pie'*
R r	*rho*	*r as in rhinoceros*
S s	*sigma*	*s as in signal*
T t	*tau*	*t as in temple*
Y y	*upsilon*	*oo as in rude*
F f	*phi*	*ph as in philosophy*
X x	*chi*	*h as in horse*
C c	*psi*	*ps as in eclipse*
V v	*omega*	*o as in oral*

ORIGINS

Modern Greek is a direct descendant of the Proto-Indo-European language, which was spoken centuries before Christ by civilizations on the Aegean Islands, on the Greek mainland, and in Asia Minor. Proto-Indo-European is the same language family from which many other European languages are derived, but Greek does not bear any close affiliation with other languages in the family because it evolved through the centuries in relative isolation. Unlike other isolated languages, however, Greek continues to be spoken today, and early written records of ancient Greek still exist.

The Greek language is believed to be one of the most sophisticated languages ever devised. In fact, Greek is the language of choice for a number of scholars and poets of many nationalities because they feel that no other language can so adequately convey meaning and beauty.

THE ALPHABET

The Greek alphabet consists of 24 letters. At first glance it may look intimidating to those unfamiliar with it, but it is actually much simpler to learn than the English alphabet. The pronunciation rules for the Greek alphabet are regular and, therefore, easier to master. Because alphabets ideally attempt to indicate separate sounds by separate symbols, it may be said that Greek has an ideal alphabet. In fact, *alphabet* is based on the first two letters of the Greek alphabet: alpha and beta.

A sign outside a butcher's shop in Skiathos, Sporades Islands. Skiathos is one of the most popular holiday destinations in Greece, thanks to its famous beaches.

English and other European languages have borrowed many words from ancient civilizations such as the Greeks. In fact, Latin and Greek are quite prevalent in English. Some words derived from Greek in our vocabulary are acronym, agnostic, autocracy, chlorine, kudos, pathos, telegram, *and* xylophone.

Sometimes the borrowed element is a root that serves as the basis for longer words. English has many such Greek roots. The following table shows some Greek roots that, combined with other words, form words we use every day:

Root	Meaning	English words
autos	*self*	*autograph, automatic*
biblios	*book*	*biblical, bibliography*
cryptos	*secret*	*crypt, cryptic*
dynamis	*power*	*dynamic, dynamite*
graphein	*writing*	*graphic, graphite*
homos	*same*	*homogenize, homonym*
logy	*study of*	*geology, biology*
micro	*small*	*microcosm, microbe*
neos	*new*	*neon, neolithic*
orthos	*right*	*orthodontic, orthopedic*
philos	*love*	*philanthropy, philosophy*
scope	*watch*	*telescope, microscope*
tele	*far*	*television, telephone*

In Greek, it is important to correctly stress the syllables of a word. A word pronounced with the stress on the first syllable may have an entirely different meaning from the same word with the stress on the third syllable.

The alphabets of all major European languages are to some extent based on the ancient Greek alphabet. The Roman alphabet (used to write English) is sometimes called the Western form of the Greek alphabet.

THE MEDIA

The Greek media exercise much influence over the population and tend to focus on sensationalist news and articles, often without regard for objective or in-depth reporting. As most of the Greek media are owned by powerful businessmen with interests in other sectors of the economy, television and radio programs and newspaper and magazine articles are filled with information promoting certain products or services. There are more than 50 newspapers in Greece with two in English—*Athens News* and *Greek News*.

In the 1980s the government gave up its monopoly over television and radio broadcasting. As a result, the number of privately owned television and radio stations increased dramatically in the 1990s. In 2001 the National Radio and Television Council, a government body set up to grant licenses to new, privately owned television and radio stations, gave authorization for 35 more radio stations to be created in Athens. Today there are 1,700 radio and TV stations in Athens.

Greek was the language in which many foundational texts of Western philosophy, such as the Platonic dialogues and the works of Aristotle, were posed; the New Testament of the Bible was written in Greek.

Greece, currently, has 19 national newspapers. One of these adopts Left Wing views (*Koel*), one is Communist (*Epohi*), another is Socialist (*Ergatiki*), one is in German (*Athener Zeitung*), and two are in English. Greece also has regional and local newspapers, including offerings from Macedonia, Crete, Athens, and Rhodes. One can also find newspapers specializing in subjects such as sports, the economy, business, and travel.

GESTURES

Body language and nonverbal gestures are a very important channel of communication. However, people tend to assume that they have universal meaning. This, of course, is far from true. One delightful gesture any visitor to a Greek home will experience is to be greeted with a hug and a kiss on both cheeks.

Greeks are eager to argue about anything, but to them, arguing is more a lively pastime than a disagreement. An important part of this activity is the amount of gesticulating that accompanies discussions. Proving that the arguments are not serious, Greeks generally calm down quite quickly after a heated conversation.

Some typical body language used in Greece:

1. *Crossed fingers, which usually signify hope or wishing for something to Americans, is the sign of two people in a close, romantic relationship.*
2. *A pursed hand gesture is a sign of excellence.*
3. *Pulling on the lower eyelid indicates superiority or disbelief.*
4. *The head tossed jerkily upward in a backward motion means "no."*

Greeks make a puff of breath through pursed lips, as if spitting, after giving a compliment. This is a superstition meant to protect the person receiving the compliment from the evil eye.

In 1994 the Greek government created the Ministry of Press and Information to handle media issues. The head of the ministry also serves as the government spokesperson. The ministry operates the Greek state broadcaster ERT, in addition to three television channels that broadcast nationwide and five national radio channels. Television and radio programmes are also transmitted live over the Internet. There were more than 7 million, 67 percent of the population, Internet users in Greece at the end of 2012.

Men debating at a kebab restaurant in Athens.

DIALECTS

A unique aspect of the Greek language is that it consists of two dialects: *dimotiki* (dee-moh-tee-KEE) and *katharévousa* (kah-thah-REH-voo-sah). Historically, *dimotiki* was the language of the common people, and it is still used in casual speech by all Greeks. *Katharos* means "pure." In the 1830s, scholars created a "superior language," *katharévousa*, based on the classic tongue. This artificial language became the official language of Greece, and everything, from laws to nursery rhymes, was written in *katharévousa*. Opposition to this "dead" language was strong, however, and in 1976 *dimotiki* was declared the official language of Greece.

INTERNET LINKS

www.omniglot.com/writing/greek.htm

This is a fascinating page on the Greek alphabet and number system.

http://greek-language.com/grammar/

This is an instructional page with links to step-by-step lessons on Hellenistic Greek.

http://kypros.org/LearnGreek/

This website contains instructional lessons on modern Greek, complete with audio files.

There were 7 million Internet users in Greece at the end of 2012, or 67 percent of the population.

ARTS

The Brandenburg Gate was modelled on the Propylaeum of Athens's Acropolis. It has a sandstone structure composed of 12 Doric columns, creating five portals. Built according to the plans of Carl Gotthard Langhans from 1788–91, the gate was commissioned by Frederick William II as an entrance to Unter den Linden, which led to the Prussian palace.

10

WESTERN CIVILIZATION IS indebted to Greece for its artistic legacy. In fact, most forms of Greek art, such as architecture, painting, sculpture, and literature, have had a direct influence on the development of the arts in the West.

After the Athenians defeated the Persian army in the battle of Salamis in 480 B.C., Athens became a center for democracy and the arts under the enlightened rule of Pericles. He not only rebuilt the city but also summoned the best artists and scholars in Greece to Athens. During this era (461-31 B.C.), known as the Golden Age, the arts flourished.

The ancient Greeks were among the earliest to separate religion from the study of ideas and knowledge—a discipline that became known as philosophy. The philosophical writings of the Golden Age have formed the basis for intellectual writing in the West. Poetry and drama also developed during the Golden Age, with epic and lyric poetry and comic and tragic drama as the most enduring forms.

The ancient Greeks created architectural styles that became models of perfection for the entire Western world. Greek sculpture of the human body set the standard for the ideal aesthetic form.

Although no original Greek paintings have survived, their beauty is described in ancient writings, and many surviving Roman paintings are believed to have been greatly influenced by ancient Greek painting.

EARLY GREEK LITERATURE

Greek literature, which dates back to the second millennium B.C., has been the most influential literary force in the Western world. From

"(I)t is the wine that leads me on, the wild wine that sets the wisest man to sing at the top of his lungs, laugh like a fool—it drives the man to dancing... it even tempts him to blurt out stories better never told."—Homer, *The Odyssey.*

the days of the Roman Empire to the present, Greek writing has influenced every literary form in Europe. The ancient Greeks wrote lyric and epic poetry, tragic and comic drama, philosophical essays and dialogues, literary letters, and critical and biographical histories that are well known and continue to be read in schools and universities around the world.

The first significant Greek literary form was epic poetry—narrative poems that described the heroic deeds of gods and men. Homer, perhaps the greatest Greek poet, composed *The Iliad* and *The Odyssey* around 800 B.C. These poems, which emphasized the ideals of honor and bravery, greatly influenced Greek culture and education. *The Iliad* told the story of the Trojan War and *The Odyssey* described the travels of Odysseus, a hero of the Trojan War. Another important epic poem was *The Theogony,* written by Hesiod around 600 B.C. It told of the origin and history of the Greek gods. One other monumental work by Hesiod is *Works and Days,* describing the lives of Greek peasant farmers.

Lyric poems emerged around 650 B.C. These were much shorter than epic poems, and they generally described personal feelings rather than acts of valor. Lyric poetry was also sung to the music of the lyre. A form of lyric poetry was the choral lyric, sung by groups and accompanied by music and dancing. The best-known lyric poets of this period were Pindar, author of the Olympian odes, and Sappho. Most of Sappho's love poems were addressed to women. The Greek philosopher Plato called her the tenth Muse, perhaps because of her direct and intense language.

Greek vase painting of the death of Hector on a Corinthian bowl dating from the sixth century B.C.. In Greek mythology, Hector was the son of King Priam of Troy and his wife, Hecuba. A Trojan hero and warrior, he fought bravely against the Greeks in the Trojan War.

THE GOLDEN AGE

Drama emerged as one of the most important literary forms of the Golden Age. Aeschylus, Euripides, and Sophocles were the three great tragic playwrights of the Golden Age. Comedy was just as popular, and the works of Aristophanes are the most famous. They reflected the spirited sense of freedom felt by the Athenians of the time and their ability to poke fun at themselves. Thanks to their masterful use of the language and complexity of thought and insight, these works of genius are still enjoyed as great works of literature today.

Prose replaced poetry as the leading literary form by the end of the fourth century B.C., and historical writings became popular. Herodotus, the "Father of History," recorded the cultural characteristics of the civilized world, focusing on the conflict between East and West. Another literary form arising during the Golden Age was rhetoric, which is the art of persuasive writing and speech. It was invented by the Sophists, a group of teacher-philosophers.

The great philosopher Socrates died in 399 B.C., leaving no written works behind. Yet, he is indirectly responsible for another influential literary invention—philosophical dialogue, based on his method of examining ideas. Socrates' teachings lived on through his students, especially through Plato, who kept a record of Socrates' lectures and founded a school in Athens. Plato's most famous pupil was Aristotle (384—22 B.C.). Aristotle contributed much to the study of philosophy, believing that "all men possess by nature the desire to know."

Illustration of ancient Greek theater from *The Illustrated History of the World* by Ward Lock (1880).

HELLENISTIC AND BYZANTINE LITERATURE

After the establishment of the Roman Empire in the second century B.C., Alexandria replaced Athens as the capital of Greek civilization. A new literary style, called pastoral poetry, had begun to develop around 200 B.C., launching the Hellenistic era of Greek art. Pastoral poetry described the beauty of nature and country life.

Prose also continued to develop. The works of Plutarch, a historian and biographer, have provided much information about this time. *Parallel Lives,* his most famous work, shows his desire for Greek culture to be preserved in the Roman world.

When Constantinople became the center of Greek culture, Christian religious poetry became the main literary form. The political climate of the Byzantine Empire restricted Greek writers' artistic freedom; nevertheless, many important theological and historical writings were still written at that time. These works continued to be written in the Greek language of the Classical period, which, by this time, was understood only by a select group of educated clergymen and scholars. Works written in the vernacular were limited to poetic romances and popular devotional writings, such as the lives of the saints.

The last literary medium developed by the ancient Greeks was the novel, dating from the second and third centuries A.D. Greek novels were usually romantic stories with complicated plots. The most famous Greek novel is *Daphnis and Chloë,* written in the third century A.D.

ART AND ARCHITECTURE IN ANCIENT GREECE

Art in ancient Greece was closely connected with the worship of the gods. Much of the art centered on the human form, as the Greeks considered the gods to have the form of perfect men and women.

Until the fourth century B.C., Greek architecture, sculpture, and painting were mainly functional. These art forms were used to commemorate athletic victories and religious events. The main role of the Greek architect of that time was to design and build temples for the gods, which were differentiated from secular dwellings by their elongated shape, at the end of which stood a large carved statue of a deity.

Decorative arts from this time were found mainly in tombs, although small ceramic sculptures and statuettes also decorated the homes of private individuals. Such grave monuments were very large vases with holes through which liquid offerings could filter down to the dead below. They had drawings of the deceased lying in state, flanked by mourners and a funeral procession.

Most of the tools used by ancient Greek artists were hand tools, with the exception of the potter's wheel, which was run by a foot treadle.

GEOMETRIC ART AND ARCHITECTURE

The Geometric period (about 1100—700 B.C.) of Greek art is characterized by the extensive use of geometric figures and other abstract forms. Small pieces of bronze and clay sculptures have been found from this period, including a statuette of Apollo. Like other pieces of this period, the statuette is an abstraction rather than a direct visual representation of the god. Geometric architecture in the form of temples can be found in Sparta, Olympia, and Crete. Only the foundations of these temples remain today.

Geometric vase depicting Greek warship 8th century B.C..

ARCHAIC ART AND ARCHITECTURE

The Archaic period lasted from 700 to 500 B.C. During the early Archaic period, temples built out of marble were erected on the Aegean Islands. Limestone temples covered with marble were built on the mainland.

Stone monuments were also created for the temples. Human figures were carved exhibiting the Archaic smile, a facial expression that was thought to be specific to humans only. Other significant artifacts from this time include vases painted with black figures and Corinthian-style vases often crowded with floral ornaments and monsters like the chimera.

In the middle of the Archaic period art drew inspiration from nature. Human forms became more lifelike. Paintings began to reflect three dimensions. Temples built during this time had six front columns and evenly spaced columns all around the outside.

Corinthian vases (earthenware) from Corinth in central Greece.

Sculpture of the middle Archaic period depicted people in action, often in scenes of battle or athletic pursuit. Beautiful vases covered in jet-black glaze and lively scenes were also common.

In the late Archaic period, a significant evolution occurred in vase painting: the emergence of the red-figure style, in which figures were preserved in red clay surrounded by a black background.

CLASSICAL ART AND ARCHITECTURE

In the early part of the Classical period (500—323 B.C.), Greece rebuilt many of the temples damaged during the Persian Wars. Temples were built in the Doric style. An outstanding example of this architecture is the Temple of Zeus in Olympia. Sculptures of this time no longer exhibited the Archaic smile; they showed expressions of both seriousness and joy, and details were kept simple. Scenes portrayed the moment before or after a significant event. The original pieces of this period are lost, but many Roman artists, who greatly admired Greek art, made copies that still exist.

The middle Classical period saw the continued restoration of the many temples burned by the Persians, and work on rebuilding the Acropolis in Athens began. A monumental gateway to the Acropolis was created, and the Parthenon was built. These examples are Greek Classical art at its finest.

Other significant Doric works

of the period are the Hephaesteion, which still stands in Athens; the Temple of Poseidon; and the Temple of Artemis. Great Ionic works include the Temple of Athena Nike and the Erechtheum.

The outstanding sculptors of the middle Classical period were Phidias, considered the sculptor of gods, and Polyclitus, who sculpted humans. Vase painting of the middle Classical period has a linear perspective that gives figures a three-dimensional appearance.

During the late Classical period, Athens lost its political supremacy, and its architecture declined. However, sculptures of that time are considered supreme examples of Classical art. Greek paintings from the fourth century B.C. no longer exist, but paintings in Pompeii and Herculaneum in Italy from the first century A.D. were probably influenced by them. Unfired terra-cotta statuettes, most of them recovered from tombs, survive to this day. They depict comic actors, fashionable women, dwarfs, and demigods.

The Parthenon in Athens served as the most important temple of ancient Greek religion for nearly a thousand years since the fifth century B.C.. It was subsequently converted to a Christian church, dedicated to the Theotokos (Virgin Mary), and later, into a mosque.

The most common architectural styles used in ancient Greece were the Doric, Ionic, and Corinthian styles. The Doric column was characterized by its simplicity and purity of line. The most famous Doric-style temple is the Parthenon in Athens. The Ionic column was developed at a later period and can be distinguished by its ornate design. Ionic-style temples can be found in Athens, Egypt, and Ephesus (modern Turkey). The Corinth column is the most ornate of the three architectural styles.

HELLENISTIC AND BYZANTINE ART

After the conquests of Alexander the Great, Greek art and architecture came under the influence of Asian arts. The arch and the vault were architectural elements introduced to Hellenistic buildings from Asia.

Small temples continued to be built Doric-style, although columns were usually in the Corinthian style. Gymnasiums, theaters, and other public buildings were built with great ornamentation. Private homes evolved from a rectangular hall to a rectangle built around a courtyard with columns.

WHAT ARE THE PARTHENON MARBLES?

Commissioned by Pericles in 447 B.C. and dedicated to the goddess Athena, the Parthenon was built by the architects Ictinus and Callicrates under the supervision of the sculptor Phidias. The original roof structure was decorated with three beautiful sets of sculpture—the metopes, the frieze, and the pediments—known as the Parthenon (or Elgin) Marbles.

The metopes were individual sculptures that depicted various mythical battles. The frieze was one long continuous sculpture that depicted the procession of Athenians to the temple during a festival in honor of Athena. The pediment statues depicted the birth of Athena and the fight between Athena and Poseidon for control of Attica. The most expensive part of the project was transporting the stone from Mount Pentelicus, some 10 miles (16 km) away.

In the early 1800s, Lord Thomas Elgin (British Ambassador to Constantinople 1799—1803) had large portions of these sculptures removed from the Parthenon with permission from the Turkish government, rulers of Greece then. In 1816 Lord Elgin sold these sculptures to the British Museum. Of the original 92 metopes (such as Centauromachy or "Battle of the Centaurs" above), 39 are in Athens, and 15 are in the British Museum. There were originally 115 panels in the frieze; 94 panels still exist, either intact or broken. Of these, 36 are in Athens, 56 are in the British Museum, and a few are in the Louvre in France and in Copenhagen.

The Greek government, under a forceful initiative started by Melina Mercouri, the former minister of culture, has requested the return of the Parthenon Marbles from the British Museum to their rightful home in Athens. If returned, the sculptures will be reunited in one collection. The Acropolis Museum opened in June 2009 but with an incomplete collection of Parthenon Marbles. The British still refuse to return the 56 panels and 15 metopes in the British Museum.

Sculpture of the Hellenistic period changed from simple forms that focused the viewer's attention on one figure to open forms that carried the eye of the viewer beyond the space occupied by the figure.

Byzantine art, which succeeded the Hellenistic period, left a legacy of important works of painting, mostly religious icons, and polyphonic chants sung in churches.

MODERN LITERATURE

During the 400 years of Turkish occupation, Greek literature stagnated. Only in areas such as the Ionian Islands, which never came under Ottoman

Interior of the Church of Panagia (Our Lady) of Asinou, built in the early 12th century. A UNESCO World Heritage site, this church is situated in the north foothills of the Troodos mountain range in Cyprus and contains fine examples of Byzantine wall painting.

rule, and Crete, Cyprus, and Rhodes, which were independent at times, did Greek literature continue to develop.

After independence in the 1830s, Greek scholars were divided about whether to use the popular spoken form of Greek (*dimotiki*) or the classical form (*katharévousa*) as the country's official language. *Katharévousa* was chosen as the official language, but the demotic form of writing gained widespread support in the 20th century.

After World War II, Greek literature achieved international recognition due to the works of Constantine P. Cavafy (1863–1933); Giorgos Seferis (1900–71), who won the Nobel Prize in 1963; and Odysseus Elytis (1911–96), who won the Nobel Prize in 1979. Perhaps the best-known Greek writer is Nikos Kazantzakis (1883–1957), author of the novels *Zorba the Greek* and *The Last Temptation of Christ.* Female writers include Lydia Stephanou and Nana Issaia.

Odysseus Elytis—Greek poet, essayist, and winner of the Nobel Prize in Literature 1979. One of his best known works is "To Axion Esti—It Is Worthy" (1959).

MODERN MUSIC

Greek music is the most representative cultural example of the blending of Eastern and Western cultures in Greece. When the Greeks gained independence from the Turks, their musical heritage included not only their native folk music but also Byzantine religious music.

One popular style of folk music, called *rembetika* (ruhr-BET-tee-cur), developed in the late 1800s. The *rembetika* is a nostalgic ballad reminiscent of Middle Eastern music. *Rembetika* is often sung accompanied by a bouzouki, a long-necked Greek type of mandolin. Because of their association with bars and nightlife, *rembetika* music clubs came under attack during the 1930s and again in the 1970s, during the military regime. *Rembetika* clubs and cafés have regained popularity in Athens and elsewhere in Greece.

Traditional Greek music and dance have been preserved in the remote village of Olymbos. The *lyra* ("lyre") with small bells attached to the bow, *laouto* (similar to a lute), *tsambouna* (a form of bagpipe) continue to be played here as they have been for generations.

One of the greatest opera singers of the 20th century, Maria Callas, was Greek. Vangelis, Nana Mouskouri, and Yanni are contemporary Greek musicians who have an international following. Contemporary laïkó, also called modern laïkó, the equivalent of techno music, is the mainstream music genre in Greece's nightclubs today.

MODERN ART

Greek folk art has survived through the centuries and continues to uphold the standards that made it famous. Greek folk artists are exceptionally skilful at fabric weaving, embroidery, and leatherwork.

Pottery developed on the islands and on the southern mainland for both decorative purposes and daily use. Greek pottery is noted for its simple, graceful forms. Copper, bronze, iron, and other metals replaced pottery in

Villagers enjoying music being played on the *tsambouna* on Sikinos Island.

northern Greece and in other areas of the country. Present-day Greek artists create replicas of ancient vases to sell to tourists.

Silver and gold jewelry were made not only as accessories for women but also as decoration for firearms, weapons, and knives. The jewels were also sewn onto special costumes. Greeks continue to practice the art of jewelry, and they also sell their creations to tourists.

The Ionian Islands developed a fine school of painting because of their freedom from Turkish occupation and the influence of the great masters of Venice. Ionian paintings are mainly religious icons.

After Greek independence in the 1830s, many artists went to study in Munich; the greatest of these was sculptor Yiannoulis Halepas (1854—1938). He is best known for his work in marble. Other modern Greek artists are landscape painters Theophilos Hatzimichael (1873—1934) and Dimitris Mytaras (1934—). Many modern Greek artists were influenced by the Romantic Movement and inspired by the geography and history of Greece. Later art influences included Realism and Art Nouveau.

Greek silver "Evil Eye" bracelets. It is common in Greece and Turkey to wear jewelry with blue eyes on them as a talisman against the "Evil Eye."

INTERNET LINKS

www.athensguide.com/elginmarbles/index.html

This is the story of the Parthenon Marbles, complete with pictures of the marbles in the British Museum today.

www.ancient-greece.org/art.html

This website provides links to photos of the myriad forms of ancient Greek art.

www.historyforkids.org/learn/greeks/literature/greeklit.htm

This website provides a concise summary of ancient Greek literature for kids, with links to summaries of various literary works.

LEISURE

Deck chairs on the beach in Anthony Quinn Bay near Faliraki on Rhodes Island. Greece's idyllic beaches are ideal for swimming and sun-bathing.

11

G REEKS SPEND MUCH of their leisure time outdoors because they love socializing. Social life is enjoyed out in the streets, and many return home only to sleep. It is common to see Greeks walking around the city with a group of friends.

Sometimes the groups look like moving parties, as they pick up old friends along the way or meet new ones as they go along.

Greeks have a word for the feeling of joy they experience when they are sitting among friends, enjoying food, wine, or coffee, and having a good time. The feeling is called *kéfi* (KEH-fee). When Greeks feel *kéfi,* they may spontaneously get up and dance.

Women playing the Mpirimpa card game at a shop in Paralimni, Cyprus.

In ancient Greece, bathing was considered a leisure activity and a social event in the town baths. Cities all over ancient Greece had specific sites where young adolescent males stood and splashed water over their bodies.

The *bouzoúki* is used to accompany nostalgic Greek folk songs known as *rembétika*.

FOLK MUSIC

Greece's musical tradition is in its folk songs. Folk music is one of the few art forms that continued to develop under Turkish rule. Regional songs evolved from matters that affected the everyday lives of people.

Klephtica (KLEF-tee-kah) are ballads sung by mountain folk that told of battles, heroic deeds, and defeats. Music played by the islanders, on the other hand, was smooth and disarming. The songs of those living in the valleys and plains told of enslaved people and their struggle for independence.

Greek folk songs mark every occasion—weddings, funerals, bedtime. Byzantine chants, often the only type of music heard by the Greeks during the years of Turkish rule, had a great influence on folk music. Despite the onslaught of pop music, folk songs remain an integral part of Greek life.

FOLK DANCING

There are more than 4,000 traditional dances from all regions of Greece. There are also pan-Hellenic dances, which have been adopted throughout the Greek world.

Dancing has played a vital role in Greek life since ancient times. Archaeologists have found that as early as 1400 B.C., dancing played an important part in religious ceremonies. A Cretan sword dance that is still performed today was described in *The Iliad*. Greek ceremonies and events, whether solemn or festive, continue to be punctuated by dances.

To the Greeks, dancing is not only an artistic form of self-expression but also a release for bottled-up emotions. If a Greek hears bad news, he or she may stand up and start dancing alone. This does not mean the person is celebrating; he or she may be dancing to relieve the sorrow or the stress.

Greek folk dances are usually performed by a group of people, either arm in arm in a line or in an open circle moving counterclockwise. The leader of

THE FOLK DANCES OF GREECE

Folk dancing is an integral part of Greek culture. It is believed that the folk dances performed today originated in the ritual dances of ancient Greece. Every region in Greece has its own local folk dance; the costumes worn for each dance also vary according to the region.

The zeibekiko *(zay-BEK-kih-koh), or "dance of the eagle," is commonly seen in tavernas and is danced alone or face to face with another person. Dancers hold out their arms like wings and slowly circle each other in a dance of combat. When one person performs a solo, the dancer moves around an imaginary partner. Often, the dancer seems to be in a trance. Spectators respect the privacy of the performer by not clapping, for the dance is meant to be performed only for the dancer and not for an audience.*

The syrtaki *(sir-TAH-kee) is the most famous Greek dance. It is a mellow, expressive dance. The* syrtaki *became internationally famous through the 1964 movie* Zorba the Greek, *when it was danced by Anthony Quinn. Another popular dance is the* hasapiko *(hah-SAH-pee-koh), or butcher's dance. Several men dance slowly, holding each other's hands, and do the same steps in a solemn style.*

The tsamiko *(SAH-mee-koh) is also called the handkerchief dance because the leader and the next dancer hold onto a handkerchief. The leader performs acrobatic stunts, using the handkerchief for support while the second dancer is holding it. This dance was widely performed by freedom fighters in the war for independence.*

The kalamatiano *(kah-lah-mah-tee-ah-NOH) is the national dance of Greece. It is a happy, festive dance that originated in the Peloponnese but is now performed throughout the country;* kalamatiano *dancers stand in a row with their hands on each other's shoulders.*

Greek men in *foustanelles* (foo-stah-NEH-lehs) perform a folk dance in a café.

the group often improvises, while the others follow the basic steps. There are hundreds of Greek dances, and they each have a name, although they are often variations of one another. The taverna, a casual restaurant, is a good place to see creative, invigorating dances.

SPORTS

Soccer, or *podosphéro* (poh-DOHS-fay-roh), is the most popular sport in Greece and the favorite topic of conversation among Greeks after politics. It is said the only time one finds the streets of Greece empty is during a televised match of the Greek national soccer team. Greece has a soccer league of 18 teams that play against one another on Sundays. Greeks are as devoted to this professional league as Americans are to Major League Baseball or professional football.

Sadly, the financial crisis has hit Greek soccer. All members of the players' union have been on strike since January 31, 2012, as the clubs have no more money to pay the players.

The second most popular sport is basketball. In 1987 Greece made its mark on the international scene by capturing the European basketball title. Since then, Greek basketball teams have won several major European trophies. As a result, the sport is becoming increasingly popular with young people and students of all ages.

HOME OF THE OLYMPIC GAMES

The ancient Greeks held Zeus, king of the gods, in great honor, and they built many temples for him, one of which was located at Olympia, in southwestern Greece. To pay tribute to him, they held athletic contests at Olympia every four years, laying the foundation for the Olympic Games.

The very first Olympic Games took place at Olympia around 776 B.C. Not only did the best athletes compete, but the finest artisans competed for distinction in their fields as well. The ideal man to the Greeks was one who could perform amazing physical feats as well as write poetry. The first recorded winner of a sports event was a cook named Coroebus, who finished first in a footrace.

Over the years, the Olympic Games became an important forum for the exchange of ideas among the leading citizens of Greece. The games became so much a part of national life that four-year periods were referred to as olympiads by the fourth century B.C. Peace reigned when the Olympic Games were held; all wars and quarrels were put aside.

As the number of events expanded, various structures were built to accommodate them—a hippodrome for chariot races, a gymnasium, and baths. Only male athletes competed, and in most events, the athletes competed in the nude. Women were not allowed to take part in the games or be in the audience. The only prizes awarded were olive wreaths.

In A.D. 393, the Roman emperor Theodosius I banned all pagan festivals and put an end to the games. More than 1,500 years later, the Olympic Games were once again brought to life.

In 1896 a Frenchman, Baron Pierre de Coubertin, revived the Olympic Games in Athens (right) after nine years of negotiations with the international community. Athletes from 13 countries competed. In the third modern Olympic Games, women were allowed to compete in archery, and by 1928 they were taking part in swimming and track events.

Greece is also home of the first marathon. After the battle of Marathon in 490 B.C., a runner was sent to Athens with news of the Greek victory. He ran the 26 miles (41.8 km) from Marathon to Athens and reported the news, then died of exhaustion. The race was created in his memory.

A car leaps up high at an Acropolis Rally in Greece, part of the World Rally Championship.

The Acropolis Rally has been held for 51 years by the Greek motorsports organization Automobile and Touring Club of Greece (ELPA), making it one of the longest-standing in world rallying.

Water sports are of great interest to the Greeks. Children learn to swim at a very early age because of Greece's proximity to the sea. Sailing, diving, and rowing regattas also draw many enthusiasts.

Automobile racing has gained much popularity in Greece during the past few decades. Thousands of spectators attend the Acropolis Rally each year, considered the toughest cross-country rally in the world.

MOVIES AND TELEVISION

Until the 1980s, Greece's broadcasting service was owned and regulated by the government. Many people complained that television programs lacked variety and that news programs were often one-sided or incomplete. In 1991 the television industry was liberalized and opened to the private sector. Today Greece has four national state-owned networks, three national state-owned digital television networks, a state-owned satellite broadcast network, and several national private television networks, in addition to approximately 150 local and regional television stations broadcasting across the country.

Going to the movies is a favorite pastime in Greece, and new movie complexes have been built in middle-class neighborhoods. They mostly show films from the United States, Britain, France, and Germany. Greek films are made on a limited budget, as they lack government subsidy. Still, several Greek films have been awarded prizes at international film festivals for their excellent content and cinematography. These films, however, appeal mostly to the avant-garde moviegoer and lack mass appeal.

THEATER

The summer season, from June through September, is an exciting time for theatrical events in Greece, which take place in open-air theaters.

One such event, the Athens Festival, has a program of concerts, dances, and ancient drama. Popular with Greeks and tourists, performances are held in the ancient Herodes Atticus Theater on the steps of the Acropolis. Another famous event is the Epidaurus Festival, devoted to the staging of tragedies and comedies written by ancient Athenian dramatists. The 14,000-seat arena dates back to the third century B.C.

The theater of Epidaurus is the best-preserved of all ancient theaters in Greece.

INTERNET LINKS

www.eurobasket.com/Greece/basketball.asp

Everything one could possibly want to know about basketball in Greece—league tables and all—is provided in this website.

www.greeksoccer.com

All the information available on Greek soccer in a single website.

www.greektheatre.gr/

This is an excellent site on ancient Greek theater, from the text of the plays to the masks and the costumes.

FESTIVALS

Floats at the Patras Carnival parade are largely satirical and inspired by problems plaguing Greece. This float features three mice hanging a bell on the cat's tail, where the mice reflect the Greek government (in aristocratic appearance) as having all the features of the political system while the cat represents the troika, holding bombs (which reads explosive economic growth) while reading the memorandums.

12

I N GREECE, FESTIVALS AND celebrations are a part of everyday life. Many of these festivals have their roots in ancient traditions, but for the most part, festivals in Greece are connected with the Orthodox Church.

The Eastern Orthodox Church adopted the Gregorian calendar (introduced by Pope Gregory XIII in 1582 and now used by most of the world) in the 1920s; since then, most Christian holidays in Greece fall at the same time of the year as they do in the rest of the world. The exceptions are Easter and Whitsun (a feast on the seventh Sunday after Easter), which are held according to the old Julian calendar, based on the phases of the moon.

Locals celebrating a traditional religious festival on Sikinos Islands.

CALENDAR OF FESTIVALS

January	New Year's Day/Feast of Saint Basil
	Epiphany
March	Independence Day/
	Annunciation of the Virgin Mary
April/May	Easter
	Feast of Saint George
May	Labor Day/Flower Festival
	Pentecost
	Anastenaria/Feasts of Saint
	Constantine and Saint Helen
	May 20: Celebration of resistance to Hitler's invasion of Crete
August	Dormition of the Virgin Mary
October	Saint Demetrios's Day
	Ochi Day
December	Saint Nicholas's Day/Christmas

FESTIVALS OF PATRON SAINTS

Every village celebrates a festival in honor of its patron saint. This is the saint to whom the local church is dedicated and the saint to whom the villagers are most devoted. The patron saint of Corfu is Saint Spyridon.

Saint George is the patron saint of shepherds, and Saint Nicholas is the patron saint of sailors.

All village communities organize their own merrymaking during saints' festivals. The celebrations begin with a mass, with many twinkling candles lighting up the church. After mass, the congregation shares in a huge meal cooked by the church council, and then the singing and dancing begin. People will go on singing and dancing for hours. Church bells peal the whole day through to inform other villages of the festival.

CHRISTMAS

On Christmas Eve, especially in the villages, groups of children go from house to house singing carols. The celebration of Christmas in Greece does not have a gift-giving tradition. Families do, however, have a festive Christmas dinner to end a 25-day "little Lent" period.

In Corfu, the full title of Saint Spyridon is "Saint Spyridon, the Keeper of the City" for the miracle of expelling the plague from the island. Saint Spyridon is also believed to have saved the island at the second great siege of Corfu, which took place in 1716.

Instead of Christmas trees, Greek homes traditionally had a replica of a fishing boat with Christmas decorations. The ship is a symbol of the economic importance of the sea to Greeks. A wooden cross wrapped with a sprig of basil is the symbol of Christmas in Greece, for the basil is thought to ward off the *kallikantzarakia* (kahl-ee-kahn-tzah-RAH-kee-ah), the mischievous trolls said to disturb the household during the 12 days from Christmas to Epiphany. They are believed to knock over chairs, put out fires, and cause minor accidents in the house. Basil-soaked water is sprinkled throughout the house to ward off these spirits.

SAINT BASIL'S DAY

Saint Basil's Day, which falls on New Year's Day, is a time for parties, presents, and good luck charms. Saint Basil is the patron saint of the poor and needy. Gifts are exchanged, and special Saint Basil's cake is served. A coin is baked in the cake to symbolize Saint Basil's generosity. Whoever finds the coin is believed to have good luck in the coming year.

A traditional, decorated boat during Christmas in Greece.

Traditionally rural Greeks go visiting family and friends on this day, and they customarily take some sand or a stone to the home they are visiting. The presentation of the sand or stone is said to ensure a good crop in the coming year. These gifts are piled up in the house for eight days before being thrown away.

EPIPHANY

Epiphany, on January 6, marks the culmination of the Christmas season. On the eve of Epiphany, priests go from house to house sprinkling holy water. In some communities, a procession of carolers follows the priest.

A very important event called the Blessing of the Waters takes place in all seaside villages and towns on Epiphany. The event is of great importance to Greek sailors, whose vessels have been idle for the 12 days from Christmas to Epiphany. The biggest blessing takes place at Piraeus—all vessels, large and small, are decorated, and a church procession makes its way to the harbor carrying a cross that is thrown into the sea. This is the signal for church bells to ring, ships' horns to blow, and warships to fire their cannons. Young men dive into the water to retrieve the cross, and the person who emerges with it is presented with gifts. He also has the honor of carrying the cross throughout the village and keeping it for the rest of the year.

Men diving to retrieve a wooden cross after from the sea during an Epiphany ceremony in Thessaloniki.

Saint Basil was one of the forefathers of the Greek Orthodox Church. He is remembered for his kindness and generosity to the poor. He is thought to have died on January 1, so that is when he is honored in Greece.

NAME DAYS

In Greece, people celebrate their name day rather than their birthday. Since most Greek children are named after a famous saint, their name day is the feast day of their patron saint. For instance, on June 29, during the feast of Saint Peter and Saint Paul, all men and boys named Peter or Paul will celebrate.

Men and women usually stay home from work on their name days, and parties are thrown for children and their friends. Adults also welcome friends to their home on their name days. A special church service is held for all the people celebrating their name day, and those honored give candy to their friends.

INDEPENDENCE DAY AND OCHI DAY

Independence Day commemorates the war of independence against Turkey. The war began on March 25, 1821, as an armed uprising. After nearly four centuries of Turkish rule, the Greeks won their freedom in 1829. Every year on March 25, the Greeks celebrate Independence Day with parades and a display of fireworks.

Ochi Day is celebrated on October 28. *Ochi* (OH-hee) is the Greek word for "no." In 1940, when Benito Mussolini, the Italian fascist dictator, demanded that Italian troops be allowed to enter Greece, the Greek prime minister at the time replied with a single word: *ochi*! War broke out between Italy and Greece, and to everyone's amazement, the poorly armed Greeks defeated the Italian army. Although the Germans eventually overran Greece, occupying the country during World War II, the Greeks still commemorate their successful resistance of Italian troops.

EASTER SEASON

Easter is the most important holiday in the calendar of the Greek Orthodox Church. It is celebrated according to the Julian calendar, and usually falls in April, but sometimes in early May. Easter is deeply rooted in the Greek heart and soul; many Greeks living in the cities return to their home village for the celebrations. The Greek word for Easter is *Pascha* (PAHS-kah).

The Easter season begins with a carnival season three weeks before Lent. On the last night before Lent, people eat and revel throughout the night for the last time before beginning the 40-day fast that marks Lent. "Clean Monday" signifies the beginning of Lent and is a day of fasting. On this day, Greeks will eat only unleavened bread and traditionally will climb a mountain to fly a kite, a symbol of release. During Lent, many Greeks do not eat meat, dairy products, or olive oil or drink wine.

Greek men and women dancing on "Clean Monday." The day marks the end of the carnival season and the beginning of Lent, the 40-day fasting period leading to Easter.

The flower festival is celebrated on May 1. People gather flowers that grow in the wild in the countryside and make wreaths and garlands that they place in their homes and hang on doorways and balconies.

On Good Friday, strict fasting is observed. Funeral services to mark the death of Christ are held in all churches. The next day, Holy Saturday, a Resurrection mass is celebrated, and at midnight, the clergy and choir chant hymns in the streets. The priest hands out the holy flame by lighting worshippers' candles and exclaims "*Christos anesti*" (Chris-TOHS ah-NES-teh), meaning "Christ is risen." Parishioners respond with "*Alithos anesti*" (Ah-lee-THOS ah-NES-teh), meaning "Indeed, He has risen."

Everyone then goes home, carrying the candles and the holy flame, as this signifies bringing home the spirit of Easter. The family feasts on soup and cakes. Hard-boiled eggs that have been dyed red to symbolize Christ's blood are knocked together. The egg that outlasts the rest brings luck to its holder. Fireworks are set off, and the feasting goes on into the night. On Easter Sunday, Greeks attend church services at dawn in their holiday finery, perform folk dances, feast on the traditional meal of roast lamb, and welcome the start of spring.

Apart from roast lamb, a traditional sweet brioche bread, called *tsoureki*, is served during Easter with red-dyed eggs to represent the blood of Christ.

INTERNET LINKS

www.greecetravel.com/holidays/

This is a comprehensive website on Greek holidays, including information about name days.

www.greekboston.com/churches/holydays.shtml

Every Greek name day is named in this website, and the holy days are listed as well.

http://carolinacrete.hubpages.com/hub/Greek-Easter

This site provides information on how Easter is celebrated in Greece, complete with the run-up to Easter and Greek Easter food.

FOOD

Fresh fish for sale at a market in Thessaloníki.

13

EATING AND DRINKING IN GREECE are not just a means of satisfying one's hunger and thirst—meals are also social events. Food and drink provide a very pleasant occasion for talking, arguing, socializing, gossiping, and making business deals.

Greeks have a culinary tradition that stretches back 4,000 years. One of the world's first cookbooks was written by Hesiod, who lived in the seventh century B.C. Literature shows that the ancient Greeks enjoyed baked fish, roast lamb, and honey cakes and used many of the herbs and spices that are still used by modern Greek cooks.

Traditional Greek breads and cookies on sale at a bakery in Kastoria.

Ancient Greek cuisine was characterized by its frugality and was founded on the "Mediterranean triad": wheat, olive oil, and wine, with meat being rarely eaten and fish being more common.

TRADITIONAL FOOD AND DRINK

Geography and climate are strong influences on the cuisine of Greece. Although Greece is located in Europe, its close proximity to the Middle East, in addition to the years of Turkish rule, have given Greek cuisine a distinct Middle Eastern touch. The Turks brought coffee to Greece, and the Persians introduced rice, yogurt, and many sweet desserts.

On the Greek mountains, herds of sheep and goats provide meat and dairy products. Although chicken and pork are eaten in Greece, lamb remains the favorite meat, and goat's milk is used as a beverage and to make feta cheese. As Greece is surrounded by the sea, fish and seafood seasoned with local lemon juice and tangy oregano are very popular dishes, especially in towns and villages close to the sea.

Greeks enjoy vegetables, such as eggplant, tomatoes, and olives. Their favorite seasonings are olive oil, lemon juice, garlic, basil, and oregano.

THE OPEN-AIR MARKET OF ATHENS

In the center of Athens, on Athena Street, there is a large market that has been thriving for decades and is representative of markets located in towns throughout Greece.

The Athens fish market is often mentioned in Greek literary texts; the market opens early and is always filled with shoppers. The floor is strewn with sawdust to soak up the melting ice. The air is filled with the smell of fish, and fishmongers noisily try to draw buyers to their stalls.

The meat market nearby has rows of whole lambs, pigs, calves, and poultry hanging on hooks. Meat vendors call out the advantages of their fine meats and persuade passersby to buy from them.

Next might be the cheese shop, where fragrant cheeses stand in huge piles while the cheese seller cuts off chunks to weigh for customers and to hand out as sample tidbits to tempt passersby. Soft and white feta cheese is the most famous type of Greek cheese. Feta has been around since Homeric times, and it is estimated that the average Greek consumes more than 26 pounds (12 kg) of feta cheese per year.

Other types of Greek cheeses are *mizithra* (mee-ZITH-rah), *kasseri* (kah-SEH-ree), *kefalotyri* (keh-fah-loh-TEE-ree), *graviera* (grah-vee-EH-rah), and *manouri* (mah-NOO-ree). Greek cheese ranges from unsalted and soft to hard, salty, and strong in taste.

Among some of the vegetables piled high at stalls in the market are eggplants, tomatoes, green peppers, okras, and assorted greens.

Markets can be found in almost every town in Greece. In some small villages, vendors go from door to door selling groceries.

Every area of Athens has at least one regular market once a week selling fruit, vegetables, and often fish and flowers too. Markets start at around 6 A.M. and finish at about 2 P.M.

A butcher at the central food meat market in Athens displays various meats hung on hooks.

POPULAR GREEK DISHES

Greeks enjoy many tasty appetizers that are served before the main meal. One of the best known is *taramosalata* (tah-rah-moh-sah-LAH-tah), a dip made of fish roe. Another dip, *tzatziki* (zaht-ZEE-kee), is made from cucumbers and garlic mixed with yogurt. These dips are delicious with either bread or vegetables.

Favorite Greek soups include avgolemono, a chicken broth with rice, egg, and lemon juice, and *psarósoupa* (sah-ROO-soo-pah), a fish broth.

Meat dishes such as souvlaki, or shish kebabs, and *keftédes* (kef-THEH-des), or meatballs, are well known in the West. Moussaka, a pie made with ground meat, eggplant, and cream, is also found in Turkey. *Dolmádes* (dol-MAH-thehs) are vine leaves stuffed with ground meat and rice. *Styphádo* (sti-FAH-thoh) is a meat stew.

Greek seafood, such as shrimp, crayfish, lobster, octopus, and squid, is usually served with a simple sauce made with lemons and olive oil. Fish is usually fried or grilled.

Meze, or small Greek appetizers, served in a restaurant.

MEALTIMES

Breakfast, or *proeeno* (pro-ee-NOH), is a light meal, eaten as early as 7 A.M. Many people have only Greek coffee, which is a strong, thick mixture of fine ground coffee, water, and sometimes sugar boiled together. This is sometimes accompanied by a roll with butter, honey, or jelly.

Lunch, or *mesimeriano* (meh-see-meh-ree-ah-NOH), is the main meal, and it is eaten at home at 2 or 3 P.M. Appetizers, meat or fish, salad, yogurt with honey, and fruit may be served at a typical midday meal. Wine, beer, and water are common drinks for lunch. In summer the midday meal is often followed by an afternoon nap, during which schools and businesses close.

AVGOLEMONO (EGG-AND-LEMON SOUP)

8 cups, strained chicken broth

½ cup uncooked rice

4 eggs

Juice of 2 lemons

Bring broth to a boil, and add rice. Cook until rice is tender, about 20 minutes. Remove broth from heat. Before serving, beat the eggs until they are light and frothy. Add lemon juice to the eggs, and beat slowly. Dilute the egg-and-lemon mixture with two cups of broth, beating constantly until well mixed. Add the diluted egg-lemon mixture to the rest of the soup, mixing constantly. Heat the soup and bring almost to boiling point, but do not overboil, or the soup will curdle. Serve immediately.

Dinner is *deipnon* (THEEP-non) in Greek. It is usually eaten in the late evening, perhaps as late as 10 P.M. But most Greeks have appetizers, or *mezedakia* (meh-zeh-DHAH-kee-ah), in the early evening, before dinner. Many little dishes of olives, cheese, freshly baked bread, and bits of grilled lamb or broiled fish are served as snacks.

Family dinners at home may consist of the lunch meal, which has been heated up, but sweets are usually served after the fruit course.

Greeks often go out for dinner to a local taverna. Rather than looking at a menu to make their selections, customers are allowed to go right into the kitchen and select from what the chef is cooking.

TABLE MANNERS AND SOCIAL GRACES

Because hospitality is considered a basic aspect of Greek culture and a natural extension of the Hellenic personality, there are no hard rules of etiquette. As in every other culture, however, certain table manners are observed:

The taverna (café) and the *estiatorio* (restaurant) are widespread in Greece, serving traditional Greek home cooking at affordable prices to both locals and tourists.

GREEK COFFEE

Greeks drink a dark, rich, finely ground coffee called kafe *(kah-FEH) or* kafedaki *(kah-feh-DHAH-kee). This is traditionally brewed in a long-handled pot known as a* briki *(BREE-kee).*

Briki *pots come in two-, four-, or six-demitasse sizes (below). Greek coffee is not made in larger quantities because the foam at the top, which is supposed to bring good luck, will not be of the right consistency. The coffee is served black, moderately sweet, or very sweet, and with a glass of cold water. Kafedaki is sipped carefully to avoid disturbing the grounds that settle to the bottom of the cup. A favorite pastime is to leave a little of the grounds in the cup, invert it on the saucer, and let it dry. Fortune-tellers can then read the future from the pattern of the dried grounds.*

- It is considered normal for dinner guests to arrive a few minutes late.
- At a meal, the male guest of honor is seated to the right of the hostess, while female guests are seated to the right of the host.
- The oldest guest is served first.
- Bread is placed on the table; there are no bread-and-butter plates.
- Hands do not rest on the lap, and wrists must be kept on the table. In informal company, the elbows can rest on the table.
- Guests must eat heartily to avoid offending the host.
- It is very common for close friends or relatives to eat from or share one another's plates.

One of the most important things that a guest can do is compliment the host and hostess on the appearance of their home. Greeks spend many hours preparing for guests and feel very disappointed if no mention is made of it.

YIASSAS

The national drink of Greece is ouzo, a clear spirit distilled from the residue of grapes after wine is made. It looks as innocent as water but has a strong licorice flavor and can have a 50 percent alcohol content. It is usually drunk straight, although some people prefer to add an ice cube, which instantly turns the liquid milky white.

Retsina, a classic Greek wine, has a very tangy resin taste. Some people believe that the wine was originally stored in casks made of pine, which leaked resin. Others say that the resin was a preservative and Greeks just grew accustomed to the taste over the years. Many believe that the resin helps in the digestion of oily, rich foods.

Before the first sip of an alcoholic beverage, Greeks always clink their glasses against those of their friends and make a toast. Usually they say "*Yiassas*" (YAH-sahs), a wish for good health.

A family meal in Greece.

INTERNET LINKS

www.howaboutsomegreektonight.com

This is a fabulous website with recipes and kitchen secrets.

www.greek-recipe.com

This is also a fantastic site with popular Greek recipes and step-by-step demonstration slideshows on how to prepare the dishes.

www.greekcuisine.com

This website provides recipes from Greek cooks and pictures of the food.

SOUVLAKI (CHICKEN IN SKEWERS)

These tasty skewers are great served with tzatziki sauce. This recipe serves four people.

1 pound (500 g) chicken breasts, skinless and boneless, cut into 1-inch (2.5 cm) chunks

1½ teaspoon (7.5 ml) dried mint

1½ teaspoon (7.5 ml) dried oregano

3 tablespoons (45 ml) lemon juice

2 tablespoons (30 ml) olive oil

2 cloves garlic, peeled and minced

2 teaspoons (10 ml) red wine vinegar

Pince of salt

Pinch of pepper

3 medium-sized bell peppers, cut into 1-inch (2.5 cm) chunks

2 medium-sized red onions, cut into 1-inch (2.5 cm) chunks

In a large bowl, mix evenly chicken, mint, oregano, lemon juice, extra virgin oilve oil, garlic, red wine vinegar, salt and pepper. Cover with plastic wrap, and place in the fridge for at least an hour to marinate. Thread the chicken, bell peppers and onion on skewers. Place the skewers in a broiler or grill, turning once, for about 10 to 12 minutes, until meat is cooked. Baste with leftover marinade once or twice while grilling. Finally, place the skewers on a platter to serve with pita bread and tzatziki sauce.

SPANAKOPITA (GREEK SPINACH PIE)

This hearty dish is popular throughout Greece. This recipe serves four people.

Filling:

7 tablespoons (105 ml) olive oil

6 medium-sized onions, finely chopped

2.3 pounds (1 kg) spinach

5 medium-sized eggs

1 cup (250 ml) feta cheese, finely chopped

1 cup (250 ml) Gruyère cheese, finely chopped

1 cup (250 ml) milk

2 tablespoons (30 ml) anise, finely chopped

Salt and pepper to taste

Piecrust:

¾ cup (180 ml) olive oil

1 egg yolk

5 cups (1.25 L) all-purpose flour

Pinch of salt

Milk or water

Heat the olive oil in a large saucepan on medium heat. Add onions and fry for two to three minutes. Wash the spinach and chop into large pieces. Put the spinach in the pan and stir. Let the mixture cook over low heat for 8—10 minutes. Remove the saucepan from the stove. Add eggs, feta, Gruyère, milk, anise, salt, and pepper. Stir well. To make the piecrust, mix olive oil, egg yolk, flour, and salt in a bowl. Knead the dough, adding milk or water until the base becomes soft. Divide dough into two. Spread half of the dough out in a baking pan. Add the spinach mixture over the base. Roll out the other half of the dough evenly and cover the pie. Bake in a 375°F (200°C) oven for 35-40 minutes until golden brown.

MAP OF GREECE

ECONOMIC GREECE

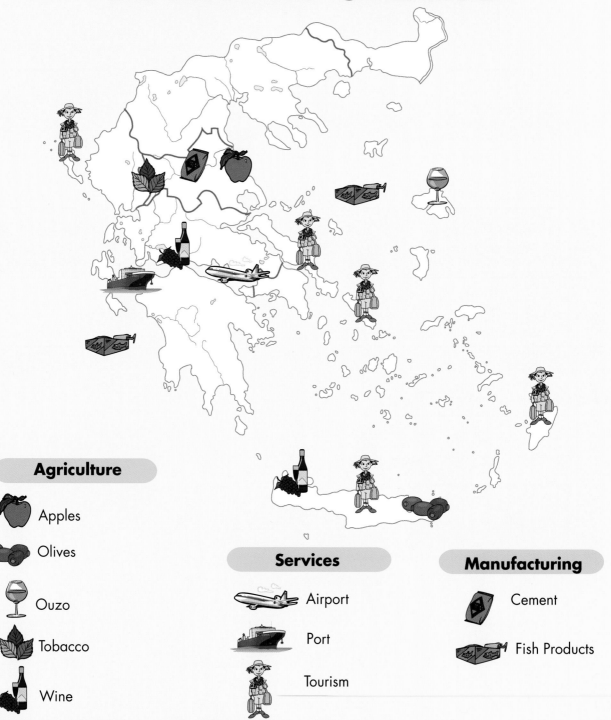

Agriculture

- Apples
- Olives
- Ouzo
- Tobacco
- Wine

Services

- Airport
- Port
- Tourism

Manufacturing

- Cement
- Fish Products

ABOUT THE ECONOMY

OVERVIEW

Greece's economy is facing a debt crisis, sparked by years of overspending and waste, and is lurching from crisis to crisis to avoid collapse. Greece has relied on international rescue loans since May 2010. Austerity measures including repeated salary and pension cuts and tax hikes have led to record unemployment, with more than 1 million people—nearly a fifth of the labor force—out of work. The country released statistics showing the recession in the last quarter of 2011 was deeper than initially forecast, with the economy shrinking 7.5 percent instead of 7 percent. The economy was expected to shrink for a sixth straight year in 2013, stagnate in 2014, and modestly expand in 2015.

GROSS DOMESTIC PRODUCT (GDP)

$280.8 billion (2012 estimate)

ECONOMIC GROWTH RATE

-6 percent (2012 estimate)

CURRENCY

The euro (EUR) replaced the Greek drachma (GRD) in 2002 at a fixed rate of 340.750 drachmas per euro.
€1 = 100 cents, $1 = €0.76 (April 2013)
Notes: 5, 10, 20, 50, 100, 200, 500 euros
Coins: 1, 2, 5, 10, 20, 50 cents; 1, 2 euros

GDP PER CAPITA

$25,100 (2012 estimate)

GDP SECTORS

Agriculture 3.6 percent, industry 16 percent, services 80 percent, others 0.4 percent

AGRICULTURAL PRODUCTS

Wheat, corn, barley, sugar beets, olives, tomatoes, wine, tobacco, potatoes, beef, dairy products

INDUSTRIES

Tourism, food and tobacco processing, textiles, chemicals, metal products, mining, petroleum

MAIN EXPORTS

Food and beverages, manufactured goods, petroleum products, chemicals, textiles

MAIN IMPORTS

Machinery, transportation equipment, fuels, chemicals

MAIN TRADE PARTNERS

France, Germany, Italy, Russia, Cyprus, Bulgaria, China, Turkey, the Netherlands, the United Kingdom, Belgium, Switzerland, Poland, Austria

LABOR FORCE

4.951 million; services 65.2 percent, agriculture 12.4 percent, industry 22.4 percent (2011 estimate)

UNEMPLOYMENT RATE

24.4 percent (2012 estimate)

CULTURAL GREECE

Pelion winter sports
Pelion Mountain was thought to be the summer residence of the Olympian gods; the town is a popular ski resort.

Thessaloníki Film Festival
The annual festival, held at one of Europe's cultural capitals, is a showcase for the work of young, emerging filmmakers in the Balkan region.

Anastenaria
This firewalking festival takes place in May on the feast day of St. Constantine and St. Helen, in Aghia Eleni, a town in northern Macedonia.

Mount Athos monasteries
Called the Holy Mountain, Athos is where 1,500 Greek Orthodox monks lead a communal life of seclusion in a complex of 20 monasteries. The first monastery was founded in A.D. 963

Patras Carnival
Highlights of the carnival, which dates back to the 1820s, are the parade of "black dominoes," women wearing a black cloak with a hood and a mask, and the treasure hunt.

Epidaurus Festival
The world-famous festival is held every year from July to September at the 14,000-seat ancient theater at Epidaurus, built in the third century B.C. The festival celebrates Greece's classical tradition with performances of ancient Greek drama.

The Cyclades summer sports
The islands of the Cyclades, such as Míkonos and Santoríni, offer opportunities for rafting and canoeing, in addition to swimming and snorkeling in sparkling blue waters and sunny climate.

Kalámata Dance Festival
Since 1995, the city of Kalámata has hosted an annual dance festival in the month of July. The festival hosts world-renowned performers from around the world as well as local dance companies.

Acropolis
Complex of ancient buildings commissioned by Pericles, of which the most famous is the Parthenon, a temple dedicated to the goddess Athena, mythological founder of Athens, and completed in 432 B.C.

Athens Festival
Ancient Greek drama, music, and dance performances are held every year from June to September at the open-air theater Odeon of Herodes Atticus. Located at the Acropolis in Athens, the 5,000-seat theater was built in A.D. 161.

Crete wine festivals
In July, the villages of Rethymnon and Iráklion in Crete hold lively wine festivals, which include music, dance, and wine tasting.

Tinos Island's icon of the Virgin Mary
Thousands of Greek pilgrims crowd the quiet town of Tinos to pay their respects and seek physical healing from the icon of the Our Lady of Good Tidings, found during excavations prompted by a vision in 1822.

ABOUT THE CULTURE

OFFICIAL NAME
Hellenic Republic

NATIONAL FLAG
Nine horizontal blue and white stripes with a white cross in the upper left corner. Blue and white represent the sea and the mountains of Greece. The cross symbolizes the Greek Orthodox Church.

NATIONAL ANTHEM
"Hymn to Liberty," a poem by Dionysios Solomos, which describes the revolution against Turkish occupation

CAPITAL
Athens

GEOGRAPHICAL REGIONS
Attica, Central Greece, Central Macedonia, Crete, Eastern Macedonia and Thrace, Epirus, Ionian Islands, Northern Aegean, Peloponnese, Southern Aegean, Thessaly, Western Greece, Western Macedonia

MAJOR CITIES
Thessaloníki, Patras, Piraeus, Larissa

POPULATION
10.8 million (2013 estimate)

LIFE EXPECTANCY
77.5 years for men, 83 years for women (2012 estimate)

POPULATION GROWTH RATE
0.06 percent (2012 estimate)

ETHNIC GROUPS
Greek 93 percent; Albanian, Turk, Slav, and others 7 percent

MAJOR RELIGIONS
Greek Orthodox 98 percent, Muslim 1.3 percent, other 0.7 percent

OFFICIAL LANGUAGE
Greek

LITERACY RATE
96 percent (2011 estimate)

NATIONAL HOLIDAYS
New Year's Day/Saint Basil's Day (January 1), Independence Day (March 25), Easter (April or May), Labor Day (May 1), Whitsun (50 days after Easter), Ascension of the Virgin Mary (August 15), Ochi Day (October 28), Christmas (December 25)

LEADERS IN THE ARTS
Theodoros Angelopoulos (filmmaker), Maria Callas (opera singer), Manos Hatzidakis (composer), Nikos Kazantzakis (writer), Mikis Theodorakis (songwriter)

TIMELINE

IN GREECE	IN THE WORLD

IN GREECE

3000–1200 B.C.
Cycladic, Minoan, and Mycenaean
civilizations flourish.

800–500 B.C.
Archaic period; city-states rise.

500–336 B.C.
Classical period; Golden Age of Athens

431–404 B.C.
Peloponnesian Wars

350–205 B.C.
Hellenistic period, under Macedonian rule

146 B.C.
Beginning of Roman rule

A.D. 395
Byzantine Empire begins.

1204
Invasion by crusader armies of Venetians,
Franks, and others

1453
Constantinople, capital of the Byzantine
Empire, falls to Ottoman Turks. Turkish
domination begins.

1821–29
War of independence; Turkish sultan
recognizes Greek independence.

1832
Britain, France, and Russia place Otto of
Bavaria as king of Greece.

1863
Danish prince William is crowned King
George I of Greece.

1908
Crete joins Greece.

1912–13
Balkan Wars. The remaining regions of modern-
day Greece are liberated from Turkish rule.

1914–18
Greece sides with Allies in World War I.

1922
Greece is defeated by Turks in Asia Minor.
Brutal population exchange of Turks and
Greeks between both countries.

1936–40
Military dictatorship of Ioánnis Metaxas

1940
Metaxas denies Mussolini's troops entry,
and Greeks drive out Italian army.

IN THE WORLD

753 B.C.
Rome is founded.

116–17 B.C.
The Roman Empire reaches its greatest extent,
under Emperor Trajan (98–17).

A.D. 600
Height of Mayan civilization

1530
Beginning of trans-Atlantic slave trade organized by
the Portuguese in Africa.

1789–99
French Revolution

1861
U.S. Civil War begins.

1869
The Suez Canal is opened.

1914
World War I begins.

1939
World War II begins.

IN GREECE	IN THE WORLD
1941–45	**1945**
Nazi occupation	The United States drops atomic bombs on
1967–74	Hiroshima and Nagasaki.
Military dictatorship by "the Colonels"	
1975	
Parliament abolishes monarchy.	
1981	
Greece joins the European Community.	**1991**
Andreas Papandreou's socialist party	Break-up of the Soviet Union
(PASOK) wins elections.	**2001**
2002	World population surpasses 6 billion.
Greece adopts the euro.	**2003**
	War in Iraq begins
2004	**2004**
Athens hosts the Olympic Games.	Eleven Asian countries are hit by gient tsunami,
2005	killing at least 225,000 people.
Parliament ratifies EU constitution and	
approves changes to labor laws.	
2006	
Public-sector workers strike over pay and	
in protest at government plans to scrap	
job-security laws and intensify privatization.	
2007	
Prime Minister Kostas Karamanlis wins a	
narrow majority in the elections.	
2008	**2008**
Parliament narrowly passes government's	Earthquake in Sichuan, China, kills 67,000.
controversial pension-reform bill.	
2009	**2009**
Opposition socialist party PASOK wins snap	Outbreak of flue virus H1N1 around the world.
election and leader George Papandreou takes	
over as new prime minister.	
2010	
Government announces second round of	
austerity measures. Eurozone countries	
approve a $145 billion (110 billion) rescue	
package for the country.	
2011	
European Union leaders agree to a major	
bailout for Greece over its debt crisis by	
channeling 109 billion through the European	
Financial Stability Facility. Lucas Papademos	
becomes interim prime minister.	
2012	**2012**
Greek parliament approves a new package	Hurricane Sandy devastates the northeastern
of tough austerity measures agreed with the	United States.
EU as the price of a 130 billion bailout.	

GLOSSARY

authoritative regime
A dictatorship; a government that is centered on one powerful figure or a small group of leaders not elected by the people.

bora
A strong, cold wind that originates in the Balkan mountains and blows to Greece from the north or northeast.

bouzouki
A mandarinlike instrument that accompanies folk songs.

chimera
A monster in Greek mythology, usually represented as having a lion's head, a goat's body, and a serpent's tail.

dead-weight tonnage
A measure of how much weight a ship can carry safely.

democracy
A system of government that originated in the Greek city-states, in which the leaders are chosen by the people they govern.

dimotiki (dee-moh-tee-KEE)
Demotic Greek, the common language of Greece.

kafeneío (kah-fay-NEE-oh)
A Greek café.

katharévousa (kah-thah-REH-voo-sah)
An artificial language, based on ancient Greek, that was the official language of Greece from the 1830s to 1976.

kéfi (KEH-fee)
A feeling of joy and celebration.

komboloi (kohm-boh-LOY)
Worry beads used to help relieve stress.

koumbara, koumbaros (koom-BAH-rohs)
A godparent or spiritual member of the family.

infrastructure
The basic public facilities serving a country, such as roads, transportation and communication systems, and power plants.

mythology
A collection of stories about the creation of the world and the lives of gods and goddesses.

ouzo
The national drink of Greece; a clear spirit distilled from the residue of grapes after wine is made.

philotimo (fee-LOH-tee-moh)
A tradition of gaining respect from others by upholding one's and one's family's honor.

philoxenia (fee-loh-xeh-NEE-ah)
The Greek tradition of hospitality.

polis
A city-state in ancient Greece.

yiassas (YAH-sahs)
"Cheers," or a toast to health.

FOR FURTHER INFORMATION

BOOKS

Bowman, John Stewart. *Frommer's Greece* (Frommer's Complete Guides). London: Frommers, 2012.

Bryant, Megan E. *Oh My Gods!: A Look-It-Up Guide to the Gods of Mythology* (Mythlopedia). London: Franklin Watts, 2009.

Dubin, Marc. *Greece Athens and The Mainland* (Eyewitness Travel Guides). London: DK Travel, 2011.

Koliopoulos, John S., and Veremis, Thanos M. *Modern Greece: A History Since 1821 (A New History of Modern Europe)*. Hoboken, NJ: Wiley-Blackwell, 2009.

Napoli, Donna Jo. *Treasury of Greek Mythology: Classic Stories of Gods, Goddesses, Heroes, and Monsters*. Monterey, CA: National Geographic Children's Books, 2011.

Tyler, Jenny, and Amery, Heather. *Greek Myths for Young Children*. London: Usborne Books, 2009.

Smith, William. *A Smaller History of Greece: From the Earliest Times to the Roman Conquest*. Self-published, FQ Books, 2010.

MUSIC

Marcians. *Traditional Greek Music—Monahi Zoume*. 100% Womon Productions, 2010.

Royal Greek Festival Company. *Greek Folk Songs and Dances,* Collectables, 2007.

Various Artists. *Traditional Songs and Dances of Greece*, Déjà vu Italy, 2007.

VIDEOS

Best of Europe: Beautiful Greece. Blu-ray, Questar, 2010.

History Classics: Ancient Greece: Gods and Battles. DVD set, A&E Home Video, 2010.

WEBSITES

Ancient Greece. www.ancientgreece.com

BBC: Primary History—Ancient Greeks. www.bbc.co.uk/schools/primaryhistory/ancient_greeks/

Embassy of Greece in Washington, D.C. www.mfa.gr/usa/en/the-embassy

GreekCuisine.com. www.greekcuisine.com

Greek language. www.greece.org/gr-lessons/gr-english/

Greek National Tourism Organization. www.greektourism.gr

Official site of Athens 2004 Olympic Games. www.athens2004.gr

Online magazine on contemporary Greece, including country profile, news, and Greek language. www.greece.gr

Lonely Planet World Guide: Destination Greece. www.lonelyplanet.com/destinations/europe/greece

Visit Greece. www.visitgreece.gr/

BIBLIOGRAPHY

BOOKS

Guerber, H. A. *The Story of the Greeks.* Chapel Hill, NC: Yesterday's Classics, 2006.

Napoli, Donna Jo. *Treasury of Greek Mythology: Classic Stories of Gods, Goddesses, Heroes, and Monsters*. Monterey, CA: National Geographic Children's Books, 2011.

Sutcliff, Rosemary. *Black Ships Before Troy: The Story of 'The Iliad.'* New York: Laurel Leaf, 2005.

Tyler, Jenny, and Amery, Heather. *Greek Myths for Young Children*. London: Usborne Books, 2009.

Williams, Marcia. *Greek Myths.* Somerville, MA: Candlewick, 2011.

WEBSITES

Ancient Greece.org: Greek Art. www.ancient-greece.org/art.html

Ancient Greek Government and City-States. http://greece.mrdonn.org/government.html

Ancient Greek Theatre. www.greektheatre.gr/

Birding, Ecotravelling, and Photography in Greece. http://greekbirding.blogspot.com/

EuroDocs: History of Greece—Primary Documents. http://eudocs.lib.byu.edu/index.php/History_of_Greece:_Primary_Documents

Greeka.com: Greece Geography. www.greeka.com/greece-geography.htm

The Greek Crisis. www.greekcrisis.net/

Greek National Tourism Organization, www.greektourism.gr

Greek Recipe.com, www.greek-recipe.com

Greek Through the Internet. www.greece.org/gr-lessons/gr-english/

Hellenistic Greek. http://greek-language.com/grammar/

A History of Greece. www.ahistoryofgreece.com/

How About Some Greek Tonight. www.howaboutsomegreektonight.com

Kidipede: Ancient Greek Government. www.historyforkids.org/learn/greeks/government/

Kypros-Net: Learn Greek. http://kypros.org/LearnGreek/

Lonely Planet: Greece. www.lonelyplanet.com/destinations/europe/greece

Macedonian Heritage: Mount Athos—The Holy Mountain. www.macedonian-heritage.gr/Athos/General/Introduction.html

The New York Times: Greece http://topics.nytimes.com/top/news/international/countriesandterritories/greece/index.html

Omniglot: Greek Alphabet. www.omniglot.com/writing/greek.htm

The Parthenon Marbles. www.damon.gr/marbles

Storynory: Greek Myths. http://storynory.com/category/educational-and-entertaining-stories/greek-myths/

INDEX

INDEX